VICTORY in T.

~

The light shines in the darkness, and the darkness has not overcome it.
John 1:5 (NIV)

~

A study of Jesus through
Matthew, Mark, Luke, John and beyond.

Your word is a lamp for my feet, a light on my path. Psalm 119:105 (NIV)

Book 4 of 4 in the L.I.G.H.T. series
(L.ife I.n G.od H.olds T.ruth) (John 8:12)

#1 TRUST in The LIGHT (John 12:46)
#2 LIVE in The LIGHT (John 12:36)
#3 REST in The LIGHT (Psalm 62:1)
#4 VICTORY in The LIGHT (John 1:5)

JANETTE KIEFFER

Copyright © 2021 Janette Kieffer

redeeminggrace991@gmail.com

All rights reserved.
No part of this book may be reproduced without written permission from the author.

ISBN: 9781736297643
This title available on Amazon.

Scripture quotations marked NLT are taken from the *Holy Bible*, New Living Translation, copyright © 1996, 2004, 2007, by Tyndale House Foundation. Used by permission of Tyndale House Publishers, Inc., Carol Stream, Illinois 60188. All rights reserved.

Scripture quotations taken from The Holy Bible, New International Version®, NIV Copyright © 1973, 1978, 1984, 2011 by Biblical, Inc. ® Used by permission. All rights reserved worldwide.

"The New King James Version" and "NKJV" are registered trademarks of Thomas Nelson, Inc. Used by Permission.

Scripture taken from the *New American Standard Bible*®, Copyright © 1960, 1962, 1963, 1968, 1971, 1972, 1973, 1975, 1977, 1995 by Lockman Foundation. Used by permission.

Scripture quotations marked (ESV) are from The ESV® Bible (The Holy Bible, English Standard Version®, copyright © 2001 by Crossway, a publishing ministry of Good News Publishers. Used by permission. All rights reserved.

Redeeming Grace 99|1 Ministries
1001-A E. Harmony Rd.
#46
Fort Collins, Colorado 80525

TO THE LION OF JUDAH, THE VICTORIOUS ONE, THE KING OF KINGS AND LORD OF LORDS

… the Lion of the tribe of Judah, the Root of David, has triumphed. … Revelation 5:5 (NIV) On his robe and on his thigh he has the name written, King of kings and Lord of lords. Revelation 19:16 (ESV) saying, "Amen! Blessing and glory and wisdom and thanksgiving and honor and power and might be to our God forever and ever! Amen." Revelation 7:12 (ESV)

…and to Bev Engeldinger

She fought the good fight, she finished the race, and she kept the faith. (2 Timothy 4:7)
…Well done, good and faithful servant!… Matthew 25:23 (NIV)

~

Brothers and sisters, we do not want you to be uninformed about those who sleep in death, so that you do not grieve like the rest of mankind, who have no hope. For we believe that Jesus died and rose again, and so we believe that God will bring with Jesus those who have fallen asleep in him. According to the Lord's word, we tell you that we who are still alive, who are left until the coming of the Lord, will certainly not precede those who have fallen asleep. For the Lord himself will come down from heaven, with a loud command, with the voice of the archangel and with the trumpet call of God, and the dead in Christ will rise first. After that, we who are still alive and are left will be caught up together with them in the clouds to meet the Lord in the air. And so we will be with the Lord forever. Therefore encourage one another with these words. 1 Thessalonians 4:13-18 (NIV)

… "Death has been swallowed up in victory." "Where, O death, is your victory? Where, O death, is your sting?" The sting of death is sin, and the power of sin is the law. But thanks be to God! He gives us the victory through our Lord Jesus Christ. Therefore, my dear brothers and sisters, stand firm. Let nothing move you. …
1 Corinthians 15:54-58 (NIV)

CONTENTS

WELCOME & NOTES

Greetings dear one,

Thank you for meeting me here. I have been praying for you and no doubt have you come to hold this study in your hands but by sheer answered prayer. Prayer that what is written here would honor Him in every way and be an encouragement to His people.

This is book four in a four book study series on the life of Jesus. If you have not had a chance to begin from the beginning that is completely fine, you are welcome to jump in with both feet right here, right now! However I would encourage you to find the other books in this series, "TRUST in The Light", "LIVE in The Light" and "REST in The Light" at some point, if God so leads you, in order to complete this studied portrait of His life story. If you have joined us on the journey through any of the other books this one will quite literally pick right up where we left off in book 3 in the life of Jesus!

This study will continue to have us dancing to the harmony of the four gospels[1] (Matthew, Mark, Luke and John) and leaping into various other books of the Bible as well because as I'm sure you have heard, the Bible really is the best commentary on itself!

As we seek to intimately know our Savior's heart through an in-depth study of His Word we will twist and turn the looking glass up into His Light for it is only in His Light that we truly see Light (Psalm 36:9). We will look at the questions and situations others in Scripture posed to Jesus and how each afforded Him another opportunity to reveal more of Who He is and wanted to be to them. In turn might we begin to see our questions, trials, setbacks, failures, triumphs and successes all as opportunities for Him to reveal more of His heart to us!

I am praying as we climb this mountain of discovery together taking on one "rock" at time we will at the end be able to look back and see that all those stones have become our stepping stones of remembrance; our Ebenezer's, each one declaring His praise that *"Thus far the LORD has helped us.'"* (1 Samuel 7:12 NIV) He is faithful!

With a trusting faith emboldened, minds captivated, and hearts enraptured by The King of kings may we never stop climbing our mountain one step at a time! To His praise and glory, when we reach the top (and you will) may you find that all those stones have added up to one giant mountain - conquered... because He said, *"'Never will I leave you; never will I forsake you.'* (Hebrews 13:5 NIV) ... remember beloved, how thus far I have always helped you."

Go back to what you know, remember your Ebenezer, your stepping stones of faith placed on the solid foundation of Jesus Christ and keep climbing, someone needs the Hope you have!

---

[1] NLT Parallel Study Bible © 2011 by Tyndale House Publishers, Inc., Carol Stream, IL 60188. All rights reserved. Pg. 1727-1731 (Harmony of the gospels list referenced.)

STUDY NOTE on "A Time to Reflect" pages:

At the end of each week a space is created for you to just sit at His feet and abide in His heart as He pieces together all that He speaks to you through your week of study with Him. Allow Him to practically apply it to your life in a tangible life changing way as only He could. I am praying He tailor fit His Word to your heart and mind so that the result is beautiful life transformation into more of who He created you to be as a reflection of His Son.

I would also encourage you to consider who God has placed in your sphere of influence that He may have you share what you are learning. The "recipe" you use to share can be aligned to your gifts, abilities and enjoyments. Do you like to take walks? If so, maybe consider using a walk as your "recipe for reflection" with another. Do you like to drink tea or fix cars, bake or plant flowers?! Use what you have where you are at. Do not miss an opportunity to intentionally create a space that you can naturally invite another into.

Follow God's lead as He opens doors for you to share your learnings week to week from His Word. Pray for His wisdom and discernment before even beginning this study that God would go ahead of you to prepare your heart to receive His Word and to fully equip you. Trust Him to provide "recipe of reflection" ideas and opportunities that will honor Him and encourage others - including you!

You shall teach them diligently to your children, and shall talk of them when you sit in your house, and when you walk by the way, and when you lie down, and when you rise. Deuteronomy 6:7 (ESV) Do this so that your children who have not known these instructions will hear them and all learn to fear the LORD your God. Do this as long as you live... (Deuteronomy 31:31 NLT)

Let this be written for a future generation, that a people not yet created may praise the LORD: Psalm 102:18 (NIV)

May grace, peace and living hope be yours in abundance~ Janette

P.S. If you happen to embark on this study with a group of people, there is a blank page at the end of the book which should allow you room to take notes or jot down encouragements, prayers and insights gained within weekly group gatherings. Meeting regularly to discuss and share collectively how God has been moving within each heart as you have met with Him individually during the week, is a great way to encourage one another in the faith. Romans 1:12 (NIV) *that is, that you and I may be mutually encouraged by each other's faith*

WEEK 1

Whoever has ears, let them hear what the Spirit says to the churches. To the one who is victorious, I will give the right to eat from the tree of life, which is in the paradise of God. Revelation 2:7 (NIV)

Day 1: Found In His Victory

Hello, I'm so very grateful God has brought you as an answer to my prayer. We are called to not give up meeting together but to encourage one another and all the more as we see the day of Christ's return approaching (Hebrews 10:25). I pray that our hearts will be mutually encouraged by one another's faith and that we would each grow stronger and more boldly confident in living out our trust in our victorious Savior. You were made to be a vessel of His victory dear one! To His glory and praise let us begin, and may we always begin in prayer that our hearts surrender fully to His leadership.

Today is Good Friday from where I sit, however we can celebrate the Truth of Good Friday (Jesus' death on the cross in our place to pay the penalty for our sin and open a way back to Him for eternity) everyday in our hearts!!

3 words - Jesus loves you.

3 nails - Jesus died for you.

3 days - Jesus defeated death's victory over you when He rose again.

3 words - Jesus I believe.

… because I love you … (Isaiah 43:4 NIV) For God so loved the world that he gave his one and only Son, that whoever believes in him shall not perish but have eternal life. John 3:16 (NIV) See, I have engraved you on the palms of my hands…(Isaiah 49:16 NIV) Jesus said to her, "I am the resurrection and the life. The one who believes in me will live, even though they die; and whoever lives by believing in me will never die. Do you believe this?" John 11:25-26 (NIV)

I don't know if you have ever taken a moment to respond to His pursuit of your heart. I don't know if you have ever decided to simply receive the free gift of eternal life Jesus is offering you. If you have, my heart rejoices that we will one day meet face to face in heaven!! If you have not, there is no time like the present to accept His free gift of life! Walk with me a bit…

As it is written: "There is no one righteous, not even one; Romans 3:10 (NIV)

For all have sinned and fall short of the glory of God, Romans 3:23 (NIV)

For the wages of sin is death, but the gift of God is eternal life in Christ Jesus our Lord. Romans 6:23 (NIV)

But God demonstrates his own love for us in this: While we were still sinners, Christ died for us. Romans 5:8 (NIV)

If you declare with your mouth, "Jesus is Lord," and believe in your heart that God raised him from the dead, you will be saved. For it is with your heart that you believe and are justified, and it is with your mouth that you profess your faith and are saved. Romans 10:9-10 (NIV)

For, "Everyone who calls on the name of the Lord will be saved." Romans 10:13 (NIV)

For God so loved the world that he gave his one and only Son, that whoever believes in him shall not perish but have eternal life. For God did not send his Son into the world to condemn the world, but to save the world through him. John 3:16-17 (NIV)

Therefore, since we have been justified through faith, we have peace with God through our Lord Jesus Christ, through whom we have gained access by faith into this grace in which we now stand. And we boast in the hope of the glory of God. Romans 5:1-2 (NIV)

Therefore, there is now no condemnation for those who are in Christ Jesus, Romans 8:1 (NIV)

If you would like to receive Jesus into your heart today for the first time, there really is no magic prayer, just speak to Him from your heart. You might say something like… Dear Heavenly Father, I know I am a sinner in need of a Savior and I believe you sent your Son Jesus to be that Savior for me. I believe Jesus, that You are God, the Son of God, that sacrificed Yourself on the cross to pay my debt so that I could be forgiven. I believe You rose again three days later and that because You live, so can I with You eternally in Heaven. Thank you, I give you my life. In Jesus name I pray, Amen.

If you prayed that prayer for the very first time Luke 15:7 (NIV) states, *I tell you that in the same way there will be more rejoicing in heaven over one sinner who repents than over ninety-nine righteous persons who do not need to repent.* I'm filled with overflowing joy at the prospect that Heaven just upped it's population total! If today you accepted Jesus as your Savior I would sincerely encourage you to reach out to another believer that could celebrate with you and help you grow in your faith along side them.

Therefore, if anyone is in Christ, the new creation has come: The old has gone, the new is here! 2 Corinthians 5:17 (NIV)

May our Lord Jesus Christ himself and God our Father, who loved us and by his grace gave us eternal encouragement and good hope, encourage your hearts and strengthen you in every good deed and word. 2 Thessalonians 2:16-17 (NIV)

To him who is able to keep you from stumbling and to present you before his glorious presence without fault and with great joy — to the only God our Savior be glory, majesty, power and authority, through Jesus Christ our Lord, before all ages now and forevermore! Amen. Jude 1:24-25 (NIV)

If you are one that had already accepted Jesus as your Savior, is there anyone you feel God has placed on your heart to share the road of Scriptures we just walked on together? Jesus came to seek and save the lost (Luke 19:10) may we never stop praying for the lost to come and be found in His victory for them too.

Dear one, thank you for your time today in God's faithful Word of Truth. I pray that the Hope of Easter will be one that we DAILY allow to rise in our hearts and minds so that we might be vessels carrying His victory out into this world, to His glory and praise.

1 Peter 1:3 (NIV) *Praise be to the God and Father of our Lord Jesus Christ! In his great mercy he has given us new birth into a living hope through the resurrection of Jesus Christ from the dead,*

Before you close for today please take a moment with God to record the one thing that made the biggest impact on your heart that you want to be sure to take with you and not forget.

_____

_____

_____

_____

See you tomorrow!

God bless you muchly~

Day 2: Trust

…Nothing can hinder the LORD from saving, whether by many or by few." 1 Samuel 14:6 (NIV)

Welcome back my friend! Maybe you are joining us for the first time in the L.I.G.H.T. series through "VICTORY in The Light" and that is just perfect timing because there is no place better to start a journey than in His victory dear one!! However maybe you are one that has been on this journey through the life of Jesus since we began at His birth back in book one in our series, "TRUST in The Light". Whether you began with us or jumped in at book two or three, "LIVE in The Light" or "REST in The Light", you are welcome here! It doesn't matter if it's week one or week thirty one for you, His Word is powerful and effective and will accomplish all that He has sent it forth in our hearts to do for such a time as this! Before we begin let us bow and pray that we submit to His leadership today and all the way through our study over the next ten weeks together.

This L.I.G.H.T series is a study of the life of Christ through the harmony of the four gospels in the New Testament. We will quite literally begin right were we left off in book three, "REST in The Light" next week. However this week we are going to take a glance back into the Old Testament! The entire Bible ties together and validates itself as Truthful. It's a scrapbook of sorts containing records of genealogies, building instructions, Truth revealing parables and all real life adventures! This week we are going to go back before we go forward to take up a picture of the victorious God He has always been, is today, and will be tomorrow!

(Okay, I know I said we are headed to the Old Testament and we are!! But first please read a portion of Scripture in the New Testament.)

Please read Matthew 1:1-17, the record of the genealogy of Christ. _____ (If you are like me and find satisfaction in a record of time well spent, go ahead and place a check mark in the blank when you have read the passage.)

This is a lot of names that may not be very familiar to us but we can't doubt for a moment that God is VERY familiar with each life recorded here by name just as He knows and cares about every detail of your life dear one. Psalm 37:23 (NLT) *The Lord directs the steps of the godly. He delights in every detail of their lives.*

In Matthew 1:17 how many generations are recorded from Abraham to David?

_____

How many from David to the exile in Babylon?

_____

How many from the exile to the Messiah, Jesus Christ?

_____

Seems to me God is on a very organized and well laid out plan (1 Corinthians 14:33). This is the very same God that holds your life dear one. What He starts He finishes (Philippians 1:6). Lets be still and KNOW (Ps. 46:10), trusting the One who says, "I know the plans…" (Jer, 29:11) to do just that and really KNOW the plans!! Let's take Him at His Word to make all things beautiful in His time for our good and His glory (Ecc. 3:11, Rom. 8:28)!

He is able!

Between Matthew 1:6-7 we see King David (who we know was a man after God's own heart (Acts 13:22) had a son named …

_____

Solomon. Solomon had a son named …

_____

Rehoboam. Rehoboam had a son named …

_____

Abijah. Abijah had a son named Asa but Abijah is were we will pick up our study today.

Please read 2 Chronicles 13:1-22. ____

How many were in Abijah's army according to verse 3?

_____

400,000. Seems like a lot until you get a glimpse of the enemies army!! How many were they up against for this battle according to this same verse?

_____

800,000!! In verse 8 Abijah is well aware of the apparent odds against them and yet where does Abijah's confidence lie according to verse 10 and 12?

_____

Abijah sees the odds, knows the impossibilities stacked against them and yet… *(vs. 10) "As for us, the LORD is our God, and we have not forsaken him…. (vs. 12) God is with us; he is our leader. His priests with their trumpets will sound the battle cry against you. People of Israel, do not fight agains the LORD, the God of your ancestors, for you will not succeed."* (NIV)

Though the odds were severely against them and from all human perspective things were impossible, they chose to place their confidence in their God, the great I AM (Exodus 3:14). The I AM possible (I-M-possible).

Hebrews 10:35 (NIV) reminds us, *So do not throw away your confidence; it will be richly rewarded.*

In this wild display of unexpected events what is recorded in 2 Chronicles 13:18 as the reason for this small (by comparison) armies victory?

_____

…were victorious because the relied on the LORD,… (NIV)

What battle are you facing that seems to hold up impossible odds against you?

_____

_____

How can you chose to keep believing, keep trusting, and rely on a faithful, good God, that is able to bring about a victory no one knew or thought would ever be possible?

_____

_____

For myself, I first need to lay down my expectations on how I think God should work and exactly how I think the victory will look in the end. Praying to take up the attitude of Jesus toward His Father in the Garden just before

He took the cross to save all who would place their trust in Him! *"Father, if you are willing, please take this cup of suffering away from me. Yet I want your will to be done, not mine."* Luke 22:42 (NLT) I have to refresh my mind with the Truth of Isaiah 55:8-9 (NIV) *"For my thoughts are not your thoughts, neither are your ways my ways,"* declares the Lord. *"As the heavens are higher than the earth, so are my ways higher than your ways and my thoughts than your thoughts.* He clearly states His way is higher, His way is better, so why fight for my lower way just because it's what I understand?!

Every time I fight the will of God I go against what is best for me.

I can't measure His love by my situation or circumstance. Feelings are just not facts so I must go back to the Word of Truth and follow some good advice to measure His love by the cross and His power by the resurrection. Someone once said, "The life of faith begins where our comfort zone ends." Letting go our our grasp on the illusion of our own control allows us to embrace His better way in His best timing. He knows things we don't and understands things we can't. He is an infinite God and we have finite minds, we will have to place our trust in Who He has proved to be in His Word. Faithful even when we are not (2 Timothy 2:13).

Therefore, since we are surrounded by such a huge crowd of witnesses to the life of faith, let us strip off every weight that slows us down, especially the sin that so easily trips us up. And let us run with endurance the race God has set before us. We do this by keeping our eyes on Jesus, the champion who initiates and perfects our faith. Because of the joy awaiting him, he endured the cross, disregarding its shame. Now he is seated in the place of honor beside God's throne. Think of all the hostility he endured from sinful people; then you won't become weary and give up. Hebrews 12:1-3 (NLT)

Please underline "because of the joy awaiting him" in the above Scripture. Dear one, in Jesus we have a joy awaiting us too! A joy too glorious to describe! 1 Corinthians 2:9 (NIV) *However it is written: "What no eye has seen, what no ear has heard, and what no human mind has conceived"* — *the things God has prepared for those who love him* — Don't give up! *"I have told you these things, so that in me you may have peace. In this world you will have trouble. But take heart! I have overcome the world."* John 16:33 (NIV)

As we close today please glance back at the verse written out at the top of todays study (1 Sam. 14:6). How does this verse and todays lesson help you gain perspective in your own battles?

_____

_____

Psalm 18:28-29 (NIV) *You, LORD, keep my lamp burning; my God turns my darkness into light. With your help I can advance against a troop; with my God I can scale a wall.*

Our God has already won the victory we are not fighting for it, we fight from it, carrying our Victor within us as believers! *You, dear children, are from God and have overcome them, because the one who is in you is greater than the one who is in the world.* 1 John 4:4 (NIV) *What, then, shall we say in response to these things? If God is for us, who can be against us?* Romans 8:31 (NIV)

Please record what impacted your heart the most from your time in His Word today.

_____

_____

_____

_____

See you back tomorrow when we will take a glance at Abijah's son Asa, and the enormous impact one act of faith can have on the next generation! God bless you muchly~

Day 3: Legacy Of Faith

Welcome dearly beloved of God. Today we will jump into the next generation from where we were yesterday. But first let's bow in prayer before we begin, thanking God that He …*is good and his love endures forever; his faithfulness continues through all generations.* Psalm 100:5 (NIV)

Please read 1 Kings 15:1-7 which gives us a birds eye view on the man we studied yesterday. ____

According to verse 3 what was the condition of Abijah's heart in relation to God?

_____

It was not wholeheartedly devoted to Him. I'm not sure at what point Abijah sadly lost his God-confidence but we can pray not to have to learn the importance of Proverbs 4:23 the hard way. *Above all else, guard your heart, for everything you do flows from it.*

1 Kings 15:3 tells us Abijah followed the sins of who?

_____

His father, however who was Abijah's great grandfather? If you need to glance back at day 2 in your study this week or back to Matthew 1:6-7.

_____

King David, who was wholeheartedly devoted to God! What does Exodus 20:6 tell us?

_____

God shows love to a 1,000 generations of those who love Him!!

Abijah may have fallen away from the faith but I wonder if there wasn't a certain boy whose faith caught fire while watching that one day his father relied on the one true God Almighty. I wonder if this certain young boy named Asa decided to side with the God of victories that day he witnessed a battle won against all odds (quiet literally 400,000 against 800,000 kind of odds); the day his father chose to rely on The Source of every victory rather than all the tangible resources around him! It only takes a spark to start a bonfire, a breath to begin a tornado, a ripple to start a tsunami! Matthew 17:20 tells us it's a mustard seed of faith that can move mountains!

Who might catch a seed, a spark of faith because they see you rely on The Victorious and Faithful One?

Please read 2 Chronicles 14 ____ and pause at verse 11 and ponder for a moment how it echos the faith his father displayed in chapter 13.

If someone were to echo your faith what do you think it would sound like?

Please continue savoring this saga through all of 2 Chronicles 15. ____

What hope do you glean from verses 3-4 and 15?

James 4:8 (NIV) *Come near to God and he will come near to you. Wash your hands, you sinners, and purify your hearts, you double-minded.*

No matter how far we have strayed God wants us back. His mercies are new every morning! Lamentations 3:22-23 (NIV) *Because of the LORD's great love we are not consumed, for his compassions never fail. They are new every morning; great is your faithfulness.*

Humble yourselves, therefore, under God's mighty hand, that he may lift you up in due time. 1 Peter 5:6 (NIV) Let us then approach God's throne of grace with confidence, so that we may receive mercy and find grace to help us in our time of need. Hebrews 4:16 (NIV)

Our God is a God who redeems, restores, renews and makes new! *For everyone born of God overcomes the world. This is the victory that has overcome the world, even our faith. Who is it that overcomes the world? Only the one who believes that Jesus is the Son of God.* 1 John 5:4-5 (NIV)

…Don't be afraid of them. Remember the Lord, who is great and awesome, and fight for your families, your sons and your daughters, your wives and your homes." Nehemiah 4:14 (NIV) *Train up a child in the way he should go; even when he is old he will not depart from it.* Proverbs 22:6 (ESV) *I have no greater joy than to hear that my children are walking in the truth.* 3 John 1:4 (NIV)

This moment is a gift fresh and new, no matter what has been, what will your echo of faith sound like today? You may be the only Bible someone ever reads.

Let this be written for a future generation, that a people not yet created may praise the LORD: Psalm 102:18 (NIV)

Please record what impacted your heart the most through your study of His Word today.

_____

_____

_____

_____

Day 4: When Everything Goes Left He Is Still Right

Hello my friend. I commend you for continuing to fend off the distractions that consume this world and battle for our time in order to still your mind and heart before your Almighty Creator. Those who honor God, God honors (1 Samuel 2:30). Please bow in prayer before embarking on today's study, that God open our minds and hearts to receiving more than we ever could on our own. Jeremiah 33:3 (NIV) *'Call to me and I will answer you and tell you great and unsearchable things you do not know.'*

Yesterday we studied Asa, one of Judah's kings. During Asa's second year as king of Judah there was an evil king of Israel named Nadab who fulfilled a prophesy God gave in 1 Kings.

Please read 1 Kings 14:1-20. ____

What could Ahijah not do according to verse 4?

_____

He could not see, however Who's vision could Ahijah completely rely on according to verse 5?

_____

Ahijah relied on God's vision in his own lack of vision. Ecclesiastes 3:11 (NIV) reminds us that God …_has also set eternity in the human heart; yet no one can fathom what God has done from beginning to end._ We will not be able to understand it all or even most things however we have One who does see, Who does know, Who does understand; we can trust Him. _I am the Alpha and the Omega, the First and the Last, the Beginning and the End._ Revelation 22:13 (NIV) _For now we see only a reflection as in a mirror; then we shall see face to face. Now I know in part; then I shall know fully, even as I am fully known._ 1 Corinthians 13:12 (NIV)

Why is such tragedy going to befall this home? (Hint see 1 Kings 14:9)

_____

This consequence did not come without warning. See Deuteronomy 28 and specifically verse 26.

So what is God's answer to Jeroboam and his wife's enquiry about their ill son? (See verse 12)

_____

And what is God's reasoning in verse 13?!

_____

This child is the only one God has found anything good in! So even though this outcome is a devastation and seemingly everything opposite from what they would have desired, it was an act of great mercy on God's part. God spared this child from the tragedy that would befall this man's household.

Please read Isaiah 57:1-2. ____

Precious in the sight of the LORD is the death of his faithful servants. Psalm 116:15 (NIV)

Death was never part of God's original plan for us and it breaks His heart (John 11). We brought death in ourselves which we can see recorded for us in Genesis 3. Yet even then God was ahead of us and working all things for our good and His glory! Revelation 13:8 (NIV) *...the Lamb who was slain from the creation of the world.* The Lamb that was slain became the Lion who triumphed! Revelation 5:5 (NIV) *...See, the Lion of the tribe of Judah, the Root of David, has triumphed....*

Please read the two verses recorded in 1 Kings 15:29-30. ____

What God says, He does. He is faithful and He is love just as much as He is justice and mercy, grace and forgiveness, healing and restoration. He is not somedays justice and somedays love. He is all, all at once. His mercy is love, His justice is love and His love is mercy and just.

We have to trust Him to be our eyes when we cannot see. We have to trust that when we pray so hard for a "right" and all appears to go "left" He is still doing right dear one. I know it is not easy but He didn't promise easy but rather His faithful and all sufficient presence with us always.

In every hard thing we have an opportunity to take up His strength and peace that passes understanding (Philippians 4:7) and fulfill our purpose in displaying His glory for all to see! We never have to walk what feels like "left" all by ourselves because we will never be left alone. We always have the sustaining strength of the great I AM available to us if we will receive it.

But he said to me, "My grace is sufficient for you, for my power is made perfect in weakness." Therefore I will boast all the more gladly about my weaknesses, so that Christ's power may rest on me. 2 Corinthians 12:9 (NIV) Don't give up at your weakness and forfeit the experience of His perfect strength.

...And surely I am with you always, to the very end of the age." Matthew 28:20 (NIV)

But thanks be to God, who always leads us as captives in Christ's triumphal procession and uses us to spread the aroma of the knowledge of him everywhere. 2 Corinthians 2:14 (NIV)

Dear one, He is with you and He is leading you in triumph! May we trust His vision because we know His heart; His heart that poured out at the cross to receive us in, to share in His eternal victory.

Please record how God impacted your heart the most from your time in His Word today.

_____

_____

_____

_____

Day 5: Keep The Faith

Oh, the depth of the riches of the wisdom and knowledge of God! How unsearchable his judgments, and his paths beyond tracing out! "Who has known the mind of the Lord? Or who has been his counselor?" "Who has ever given to God, that God should repay them?" For from him and though him and for him are all things. To him be the glory forever! Amen. Romans 11:33-36 (NIV)

"I do believe; help me overcome my unbelief!" Mark 9:24 (NIV)

Welcome and well done dear one!! You made it to the end of week one! I hope you are feeling as saturated with Truth and Living Hope as I am! Let's finish strong today as we bow before the One who is our strength. Psalm 105:4 (NIV) *Look to the LORD and his strength; seek his face always.*

One of the enemy's age old weapons against us is to try and get us to doubt Gods character. It's easy to slip into that lie when our situations and circumstances are less than desirable and our feelings are floating on cope rather than Hope.

Thankfully from our vantage point we have the entirety of God's Word at our fingertips to elevate our perspective from our own little slice of pie to see a bigger picture of the higher story God has been writing all along! A story of victory dear one, let's take a look!

Today we are going to begin at the beginning in Genesis and make our way into the New Testament where we will predominately spend the rest of our study. I'm praying God prepare our hearts to recognize His faithful character in and through all situations and circumstances in Scripture so that we can apply that Truth to our own lives and truly live in the victory He wants for us.

Please read Genesis 3. ____

Right there in verse 1 Satan starts in with planting the seed of questioning God's Word! *"Did God really say…"* (NIV) When we feel that seed of doubt we need to run fast as we can back to the totality of God's faithful Word. *All Scripture is God-breathed and is useful for teaching, rebuking, correcting and training in righteousness, so that the servant of God may be thoroughly equipped for every good work.* 2 Timothy 3:16-17 (NIV) Please underline "thoroughly equipped" and "every good work" in that verse. *Thoroughly* and *every* are pretty confident words concerning the Word's ability to combat the enemy's attacks! How often would you say God's Word is the first resource you pick up or run to when you feel the enemy attack or the seeds of doubt thrown your way?

In Genesis 3:4 we see Satan twist the Truth. He does this to Jesus (See the temptation in the wilderness in Matthew 4:1-11.) however Jesus knew Truth so well that the twist was obvious. How well do we know Truth?

Satan tells Eve what, in Genesis 3:4-5 to get her to doubt God's character?

_____

_____

Eve sets her eyes on the temptation rather than Truth and she falls hard and brings her husband down with her. Sin is infectious like that. 1 Corinthians 15:33 (NIV) *Do not be misled: "Bad company corrupts good character."*

In Genesis 3:6 Eve sets her mind and eyes on the wrong thing and decides she knows better than God. It matters where we set our minds. Read Romans 8:5-6. ___ The mind governed by the flesh leads to what?

_____

What we set our minds on begins to form our emotions and typically we act on emotions. So we must set our mind on TRUTH. The Truth found in God's faithful Word regardless of what our current circumstances may appear to be in our finite minds understanding of things.

We see in this chapter God WAS truthful! Because Adam and Eve ate from the tree of the knowledge of good and evil they were no longer able to eat from the tree of life and live forever. Enter: death. This broke God's heart but He honors our choice and our sinless holy God cannot be in the company of sin. The garden of paradise was blocked off and yet even in banishment, God spoke of hope.

Satan's head would be crushed. Colossians 2:15 (NIV) *And having disarmed the powers and authorities, he made a public spectacle of them, triumphing over them by the cross.*

Jesus took the cross and rose again defeating the victory of death over us and making a way back, by His blood, into His presence - paradise! …*To him who loves us and has freed us from our sins by his blood…* Revelation 1:5 (NIV)

Let's jump into the New Testament now to a passage found in Matthew 11:1-6. ___

You may remember from our past studies if you have been traveling with us awhile that John the Baptist was a miracle birth, born to parents well past the childbearing age but nothing is impossible for God. John was the one to prepare the way for Jesus, he actually baptized Jesus and got to see the heavens rip open and hear the audible voice of God Himself! Check out Matthew 3:13-17. ____

So does it surprise you even a little bit that John begins to doubt who Jesus is when his own situation goes south and he finds himself sitting in prison?! Do not let the enemy outwit you!! 2 Corinthians 2:11 warns us about not letting the enemy outwit us! We are not unaware of his schemes! When things go south look up! Seek Truth as depicted in God's Word! This is what Jesus points John back to when his disciples come to relay John's doubt to Jesus.

Match Matthew 11:5 up with the Word John would have known back in Isaiah 35:4-5 and Isaiah 61:1. What similarities do you see?

_____

_____

God is faithful and His Word is our roadmap. Go back to what you know is Truth to find your faith in all that you do not understand.

Please record Matthew 11:6 below.

_____

We will be blessed if we do not become offended by the way He chooses to do things. We do not have the big picture and even if we did we would probably not understand it this side of heaven anyway. We must trust and believe the One who knows the plans, the good plans (Jer. 29:11). We don't want to be caught fighting God thinking we know better like Adam and Eve.

One more Scripture for today and we will only touch on it as we will get to dive more in-depth with it later in our study. Please read Luke 23:39-43. ____

Here we see two criminals respond to Jesus very differently in the hour of their greatest trial. One thinks he knows better than God. If God was God why would He not get off the cross and get him out of his predicament as well!?!! This criminal did not understand the bigger picture, Jesus' higher purpose. Jesus stayed to defeat sin, death and the devil once and for all, for all of us.

The other criminal didn't understand the bigger picture either. However in humble submission and reverence for God Himself, this criminal bowed his will to God's. He trusted it was better and right, even if he couldn't fully understand it.

Please record Jesus' response to this second criminal in Luke 23:43 below.

...*blessed are those who have not seen and yet have believed.*" John 20:29 (NIV) We will be blessed if we surrender our will to His, keeping the faith, trusting His way is best even when we don't see or understand it all. *And without faith it is impossible to please God, because anyone who comes to him must believe that he exists and that he rewards those who earnestly seek him* Hebrews 11:6 (NIV)

Dear one, I'm praying for you, please pray for me too that in all situations and circumstances we would not let the enemy outwit us but would be wise to his schemes. That we would saturate our minds and hearts in Truth and by the power of the Holy Spirit stand firm in our faith even when, even if, even though, because we believe the Way, the Truth and the Life is Jesus Himself (John 14:6). Then one day we will be in Paradise with Him for all eternity!

Keep the faith in the One who is and has been faithful through the ages from Genesis to Revelation, yesterday, today and forever (Hebrews 13:8). Keep the faith in the One who is keeping us in His victorious right hand! *For I am the Lord your God who takes hold of your right hand and says to you, Do not fear; I will help you.* Isaiah 41:13 (NIV)

Thank you muchly for this week in His Word. May He richly reward your hearts pursuit of His. Please record one thing that impacted you from your time today.

Day 6 & 7: A Time To Reflect

Over the next two days take time to reflect over your week of study. Maybe you need some time to catch up on the study material and this might be the perfect break to do just that with the Lord!

I encourage you to glance back at the final point at the end of each day that you recorded having had the greatest impact on your heart. As you spend time with God in prayer, reflect and record on the lines below how God is tying it all together and applying it to your life.

Ask that God make it clear who He would have you invite into a natural opportunity to share Him, to apply what you are learning. Trust Him to continue to take the lead. May we have a heart ever ready with eyes and ears out to the opportunities God wants to invite us into for His glory and praise.

Do not merely listen to the word, and so deceive yourselves. Do what it says. Anyone who listens to the word but does not do what it says is like someone who looks at his face in a mirror and, after looking at himself, goes away and immediately forgets what he looks like. But whoever looks intently into the perfect law that gives freedom, and continues in it - not forgetting what they have heard, but doing it - they will be blessed in what they do. James 1:22-25 (NIV)

Philippians 4:13 (NIV) *I can do all things through him who gives me strength.*

John 14:26 (NIV) *But the Advocate, the Holy Spirit, whom the Father will send in my name, will teach you all things and will remind you of everything I have said to you.*

WEEK 2

Whoever has ears, let them hear what the Spirit says to the churches. The one who is victorious will not be hurt at all by the second death. Revelation 2:11 (NIV)

Day 1: While You Can

Welcome friend. This week we will pick up in our journey through the life of our Savior Jesus Christ as we follow Him through the gospels (Matthew, Mark, Luke and John). Let's hold onto the victorious hope of who we discovered Him to be throughout the ages last week as we embark forward not just in study but in life. He is a good God working out His plan of salvation for us all as He prepares all the world for His second coming!

Speaking of coming, I'm very grateful you have kept coming! I'm so very grateful to have you along with me on this quest to go deeper into our Saviors heart. I do wish I knew your name though. I just met a new friend on the trail I like to walk on behind my home today and her name is Dottie. She always has the friendliest kind of smile. Then there is Jane who I see often walking along that same trail. We really know nothing about one another except each other's names and a few bits and pieces we have exchanged over time in our brief passings by. Sometimes it's just a heartwarming glance and a friendly "hello" with a smile that sparkles genuinely within someone's eyes, that fills a heart to overflowing don't you think!

Jesus knows your name my friend as He knows mine. El Roi, Hagar calls Him in Genesis 16:13, the God who sees me. El Roi is the God who sees you too and knows your name. You belong. May we lift His name high while we still can, so that others may know the love of the God who sees them too.

Let's bow before the God who sees us and ask that He open our eyes to see both physical and spiritual Truth; to see the wonders of His presence all around us.

Please meet me on the other side of John 12:20-50. _____

These Greeks probably approached Philip because although he was a Jew he had a greek name. Name a characteristic in someone else that makes them feel approachable to you?

_____

What about you, do you think, makes you approachable?

_____

As the Greeks were brought into connection with Jesus we can see that His ministry to the Jews alone was now taking on the wider world. We see this in verse 26 (NLT) when Jesus says, *Anyone who wants to serve me must follow me...* This call to anyone in the whole world is also in John 3:16. As familiar as you may be with that verse I encourage you to go to that passage and read it as if it were the first time and insert your name for the word "world" and then that of someone you pray will come to a saving relationship with Jesus, to know this Truth for themselves.

In John 12:24 what does Jesus say needs to happen in order for there to be a harvest of new life?

_____

Jesus was illustrating His death in order to bring all who would believe in Him into His Kingdom for eternity!

What did Jesus say was the condition of His soul over this fact in verse 27?

_____

What then motivated Jesus to continue forward? Because He didn't have to.

_____

As much as Jesus' flesh wanted to pray "Father, save me from this hour!" (vs. 27 NIV) He submitted, He fell to the ground offering His life for ours and chose instead to pray, "Father, glorify your name." (vs. 28 NIV) What does John 12:32 tell us happens when His name is lifted up; when His name is glorified?

_____

He draws all people to Himself! Hallelujah! It doesn't rest on our shoulders to be good enough, we just need to lift up His name and He does the life changing work inside someone!

Is there any prayer in your life that maybe needs to change from, "Save me from this hour!" to "Father, bring glory to your name." for the sake of someone else who is lost and needs to see Him lifted high through your obedient death-to-self-will?

_____

_____

This is hard, so hard. Jesus tells us His soul was deeply troubled. His mission was harder than any of us could/can comprehend. But He took the worst, so that in our worst, we wouldn't end that way because He rose again! He rose again victorious over the grave! We end in life beginning! That's Living Hope.

Living Hope is lifted up for all to see when we surrender, choosing death to self that He who gave Himself that we might live, would be glorified.

For we do not have a high priest who is unable to empathize with our weaknesses, but we have one who has been tempted in every way, just as we are--yet did not sin. Hebrews 4:15 (NIV)

What is God the Father's response to God the Son in John 12:28?

_____

This is the third time God the Father is recorded speaking aloud to God the Son. The first time is at Jesus' baptism in the beginning of His ministry. Please see Matthew 3:17 and record it here.

_____

The second time is in the middle of His ministry in Matthew 17:5 on top of the Mountain of Transfiguration. Moses, Elijah and Jesus meet on the mountain top. These men from the Old Testament represent the law and the prophets confirming Jesus as the promised Messiah. God's voice confirms Jesus' authority.

Please Record Matthew 17:5 here.

_____

In John 12:28 near the end of His ministry God the Father speaks for a third time. Each time God speaks it is during a time Jesus is confirming His obedience to the Father's mission. If we too are longing to hear the Father's voice resonate within us we may just hear it best in humble submission to carrying our cross for Him; the One who carried ours all the way to hell so we would never have to go that far.

John 12:35 (NLT) states, ...*Walk in the light while you can, so the darkness will not overtake you....*

Please underline the phrase, while you can. None of us is guaranteed another moment and none of us knows the day or hour that will be our last. Today is the day to choose to walk in the Light, to surrender to His leading and live, truly live in His victory!

Please record what stands out to your heart the most from your time in His Word today.

_____

_____

_____

_____

Day 2: Forgiveness & Fruitfulness

Hi! Today we are going to jump on over to Matthew and Mark. Let's begin in prayer asking for God's help to gain more of His Truthful perspective that we might live as a clearer reflection of His Son.

Please proceed on to reading Matthew 21:18-22 _____ and Mark 11:12-14, 20-25. _____

What time of day was Jesus up and hungry (Matt. 21:18)?

_____

Do we wake up with a hunger for Jesus? Is He first on our list to satisfy our cravings?

Please record Psalm 90:14.

_____

_____

List 2 ways that you already do, or can start to do, to choose Him first to satisfy your hearts deepest desires.

_____

_____

Matthew seems to have compressed the story compared to Mark's rendition over two days. Symbolically the cursing of the fig tree represents God's judgment on Israel due to rejecting the Messiah. Though it looked promising the lack of fruit or evidence of faith in ones life cannot be hidden. Authentic faith naturally produces acts because faith works!

Checking all the right boxes, getting to church on time, attending the Bible study and going to the Christian school, does not prove to make a heart pure. Connecting to all the "right" groups can be helpful and good but does not naturally produce a right heart. Only a heart connected to God's heart is made fruitful, pure and right.

John 15:5 tells us a branch on the vine will produce fruit. Cut from the vine that branch is nothing and can produce nothing. However when that branch is attached, nutrients from the vine flow naturally through to the branches, thus fruit appears! If we focus on abiding in Jesus, He will produce good works or fruit from our lives naturally. John 15:5 (NIV) *"I am the vine; you are the branches. If you remain in me and I in you, you will bear much fruit; apart from me you can do nothing.*

What is the disciples question in Matthew 21:20?

_____

How did the tree wither so quickly? To which Jesus goes on to explain having faith without doubt. What happens to someone who steps from the rock of faith into the sea of doubt? See James 1:6.

_____

_____

If we are not connected to the Vine we immediately begin not living! We were not made with a spirit of fear (2 Tim. 1:7), we can choose faith in the face of doubt. Jesus knows what we are up against, when you feel a wave of doubt rolling in, confess it and ask that His hand steady your faith as you choose to fix your eyes on Him the perfecter of your faith. Please record Isaiah 41:13 below.

_____

_____

That is one to tuck into your heart's pocket for sure!

Matthew 21:22 is not a promise to receive anything we want like a genie in a bottle. Rather the stronger our relationship with Him is, the more likely our will, will actually be in harmony with His heart. When we ask for that which is in the Father's will, in harmony with His heart, we can be sure to delight in His response because we've already delighted in His heart. Psalm 37:4 (NIV) _Take delight in the LORD, and he will give you the desires of your heart._

What is the one thing mentioned in Mark 11:25 we should be mindful of before praying for something?

_____

Check for any unforgiveness in our hearts. Confess anything that would come between you and the Father first before requesting something is key. He is faithful to forgive the sorry. We can come boldly before the throne but must also come humbly in holy fear respecting all that it cost for us to approach His throne in confidence. One way that we show that is by confessing any wrong in our heart and our humble need of Him as our Savior to make us clean.

Let's do this while we still can as often as needed, none of us knows how long we have left or when Jesus will return. We want to be found in pure fruitful faith.

Please take a moment to record the point of greatest impact to your heart as you studied today.

_____

_____

_____

_____

Day 3: Go For Your Anchor

Hello friend, are you as ready as I am to embark on our quest today?! Let us praise Him in prayer as we begin to step into His faithful Word. *You thrill me, LORD, with all you have done for me! I sing for joy because of what you have done.* Psalm 92:4 (NLT)

Let's dive right in on Matthew 21:23-27 _____, Mark 11:27-33 _____, and Luke 20:1-8. _____

Jesus' authority was questioned. Jesus questioned back to afford the religious society a moment to check their own beliefs.

Have you ever experienced a dilemma or trial that revealed your true heart on a matter? Please read 1 Peter 1:7 and share a time you were fire refined if you feel comfortable.

_____

_____

Sometimes trials force you to realize what your faith is worth. Whose authority do you bow to truly. Your actions under fire will prove your faith genuine or not.

There will be times when you are questioned and when you feel the waves of doubt begin to sway your boat, don't jump ship rather go for your Anchor! Find out what God's Word of Truth has to say. Evaluate the questions against His faithful Word and not the faulty, fluctuating and swaying standards of the world.

Hebrews 6:19 (NIV) *We have this hope as an anchor for the soul, firm and secure….* When your faith is put to the test, when you are questioned as to whose authority you bow to, what will your life prove?

Before proceeding please take a moment to read Ephesians 6:10-18 on the Armor of God. ____

The apostle Paul said in 2 Corinthians 12:6 that he wanted others to judge him not on all his high credentials but rather simply on what they saw and heard of him. What do people see and hear through us? Is it a picture of Jesus?

While our hearts still have a beat and our lungs still have a breath; while we still can… may our lives lift His high and bring Him glory.

It is written: "'As surely as I live,' says the Lord, 'every knee will bow before me; every tongue will acknowledge God.'" Romans 14:11 (NIV) *and every tongue acknowledge that Jesus Christ is Lord, to the glory of God the Father.* Philippians 2:11 (NIV)

Please record the point of greatest impact today.

_____

_____

_____

_____

Day 4: Dress For Success

Hello! Well today as you can see is titled dress for success. You've heard that saying before, I'm sure. Interestingly enough I recently got a new white t-shirt of which I wore for the first time today! However I am no longer wearing it because I thoroughly enjoyed a lemon ice-cream cone on my backyard swing. Swinging, lemon ice cream, white t-shirt… can you see where this is going?! Clearly I was not dressed for success or I would have been in something more of a lemon yellow shade! When I say I thoroughly enjoyed my ice cream I thoroughly mean it for I enjoyed it all down the front of my new white t-shirt! (It's now in the laundry room being bleached.) I may need this lesson more than most so let's just bow before the One who has an infinite amount of grace no matter how many "lemon" experiences we go through!

Alright dear one, please meet me on the other side of Matthew 21:28-32. _____

This is the first of three parables in a row we will look at that point out the guilt of those that reject the Messiah and the reception and reward of those who accept Him.

Who does Jesus mention in verse 32?

_____

What does He say about John?

_____

Jesus says John the Baptist showed the right way to live.
How did people respond to John according to this same verse?

_____

Jesus, God Almighty commends John, remembers John, remembers the way John LIVED out the right example. Not only that, but He also recalls the hardship and ridicule John endured.

Jesus shows no favoritism (Rom. 2:11). Do you know He remembers you, knows your struggles, commends you for your stamina and perseverance in the trial. You matter to Him. He sees you, has not forgotten you. Revelation 2:2 (NLT) states, *"I know all the things you do. I have seen your hard work and your patient endurance. …* Verse 3, *You have patiently suffered for me without quitting.*

Take heart, He sees you, remembers you, and is with you even now, take His Word and receive His peace.

Show me your ways, Lord, teach me your paths. Guide me in your truth and teach me, for you are God my Savior, and my hope is in you all day long. Psalm 25:4-5 (NIV)

Let's move to another grouping of Scriptures today, found in Matthew 21:33-46 _____, Mark 12:1-12 _____ and Luke 20:9-19. _____ We will take the rest of today and tomorrow to fully digest these passages.

This parable draws on Isaiah 5:1-7. Go ahead and read that for context as well. The religious leaders of that time would have known and recognized the correlation between the passage in Isaiah and this current parable Jesus told. The religious leaders were aware that the passage in Isaiah addressed the wicked leadership of God's chosen nation Israel. What question does Isaiah 7:4 ask?

_____

Clearly God did everything possible for His people and still they bore bitter fruit. Can you think of a time you tried everything in your power and still nothing seemed to work like you pictured in your mind?

_____

_____

God understands the disappointment of unmet expectations, like when you expect "sweet grapes" and you end up with "bitter grapes" instead.

It's a disappointment to bear for sure however our God is never without a plan. In fact no amount of bitter fruit can thwart His plan for all of humanity or for your individual life either. What comfort does knowing that no matter how many times our human plans fall apart His plan for our lives just can NOT fall apart! Reflect below. (Job 42:2)

_____

_____

Back to our parable first listed in Matthew 21:33-46. The landowner resembles God and the vineyard is the nation of Israel. The tenant farmers are the religious leaders while the landowners servants represent the faithful prophets and priests. The son is Jesus and the other tenants are the Gentiles.

Can you identify the way Jesus is exposing the religious leaders' evil plot to kill Him? Psalm 139:2 tells us He knows our thoughts even before we think them! We will never out-think God or come up with some idea He has not already derived. How does this embolden your trust to know He is always in the know and always before us in thought, word and deed?

_____

Psalm 37:23 (NLT) *The LORD directs the steps of the godly. He delights in every detail of their lives.*

What question does Jesus ask AGAIN in Matthew 21:42?

_____

It's almost comical how many times Jesus has asked the leaders of that time (that knew the Scriptures frontwards and backward) in multiple situations, with almost flabbergasted disbelief, if you can just imagine it ... *"Didn't you ever read this in the Scriptures?"* Matt. 21:42 (NLT)

We too have the very God breathed Word of God at our fingertips every day here in the US with the freedom to read it outright and with friends!! How often do we take advantage of that?! How much do we reverence such a privilege?!! What are we doing to magnify such a glorious privilege and opportunity to those around us? How are we intentional about not just KNOWING it like the religious leaders of that time but allowing it to change us in the depths of our heart so that we are DOING what His Word says? Take a moment to reflect.

_____

_____

Let's put a bookmark right here in the Scriptures for today and record so far the one thing that has made the greatest impact on your heart from your study today.

_____

_____

_____

_____

Day 5: Dress For Success (part 2)

Welcome back! We are going to dive right back into our Scriptures that we started in yesterday. Please begin in prayer and then if needed go ahead and refresh your mind for contest by rereading Matthew 21:33-46. ____

In Matthew 21:42 the Scripture Jesus is referencing is found in Psalm 118:22-23 please go there and record one verse further, verse 24 on the lines below.

_____

_____

The cornerstone might be or could be either the first or last stone laid. The foundation stone (first) or the capstonc (last) like in an archway. Our God is both the first and the last, the Alpha and Omega! Revelation 22:13 (NIV) *I am the Alpha and the Omega, the First and the Last, the Beginning and the End.*

He has the victory dear one! What He starts He finishes and that includes His plans for your life and my life!! Oh to take that Truth in is a day to rejoice indeed!! Each day is a new day that He has made, He is in charge beginning to end, it doesn't rest on our shoulders to figure it out, to work it out. Our job is obedience. Our job is to listen, to abide in Him through His Word and prayer. He is our unshakable Rock the Cornerstone our Capstone the First and Last, so rejoice!

Trust is the key! I know I like to think the key is knowing the plan and all the steps and checking all the boxes just so, but the longer I walk with Him the more apparent it becomes that trying so hard only finds me with lemon all over my new shirt! It's not about trying harder but trusting farther; farther than I can see on my own, farther than I can go or even know on my own. Trust is the key to a deep love relationship and that is what He's after... He's after your heart and His romance only ends in happily ever after!

Matthew 21:44 issues a grave warning. What is it?

_____

We are to build our lives on the foundation of His Truth. Some will trip over the Rock of who He is, choosing not to accept Him. In the end He will honor everyone's choice and those that have not chosen to accept the Truth will find themselves crushed. We must choose now while we can and magnify the Truth of Him for others while they still can choose too!

Speaking of the ultimate romance being found in Christ, please read Matthew 22:1-14. _____

Have you ever planned your heart out for something, someone, or an event that was just really special to you only to have little response from those you poured out for?!

We have a Savior who also knows every level of our pain and then every other level we will never have to experience as well! Oh how much unfathomably more pain and rejection our Savior, God Almighty has experienced! He who called every living thing into being by His Word yet chose to give His life to extend the invitation to eternity with Him, to give us a seat at His banqueting table... oh how much more pain He has experienced! He plans eternal life instead of hell for us at the cost of His Son's life and some turn their noses up at the invitation even still.

Who is extended the invitation once the original guests reject? (See Matthew 22:10)

_____

Has experiencing rejection ever caused you to open your eyes to a new perspective, opportunity or a new relationship(s) you may not ever have noticed had it not been for the rejection?

_____

No one in Christ ends in rejection! What new opportunities might you have around you to invite or include someone new?

_____

What was noticed in Matthew 22:11?

_____

Someone not in party attire! These wedding clothes represent the righteousness of Christ needed to enter into Heaven. The robes of righteousness are offered to everyone. It's up to each individual to put Him on, accept His sacrifice and be covered by His atoning blood.

Isaiah 61:10 (NIV) *I delight greatly in the Lord; my soul rejoices in my God. For he has clothed me with garments of salvation and arrayed me in a robe of his righteousness, as a bridegroom adorns his head like a priest, and like a bride adorns herself with her jewels.*

Notice that none of this is something we can conjure up on our own. This type of clothing can only come from Christ, thus our righteousness is only in Christ. We could never be good enough or do enough to earn it. Redemption is a free gift purchased by His blood. We must only accept it to be dressed for ultimate success.

Our final portion of Scriptures for today will be in Matthew 22:15-22 _____, Mark 12:13-17 _____ and Luke 20:20-26. _____

In these passages the Pharisees were trying to trap Jesus into saying something so that they could have a reason to arrest Him. They sent people to act friendly at first stating they knew He was honest and truthful and that He didn't play favorites. All this is true of Jesus but their hearts were not in their compliments they were acting hypocritically and Jesus knew it. Have we ever found ourselves worshiping/praying/serving Him in a hypocritical manner?

Psalm 139:23-24 _____

I'm pretty sure the clothing doesn't come in hypocritically size so we would all do well to submit to a bit of holy soul searching by our heavenly Father. Responding in humility, repenting of anything He finds and brings to light so that we can lose that weight that so easily entangles. We don't want to be found needing alterations once it's too late!

What does Jesus ask about the coin, in Matthew 22:20?

_____

He asks about the image on it. The image on the coin is Caesars, so who does Jesus say it belongs to?

_____

Caesar.

Record what Genesis 1:27 states in your own words and also notice how many times in that one verse it is stated!

_____

Three times the fact that we are made in His image and that He is our Creator is repeated so undoubtedly who do we belong to?

Dear one, you were made in His image! Having accepted Jesus as your personal Savior you belong at the banquet. You belong in His family, you are His child. Don't let this world tell you otherwise no matter how many well planned events go unattended! Keep going, don't give up, your Alpha and Omega are waiting with the best dressed outfit you will ever wear! You are going to be stunning!

In the meantime He holds out advice on how to dress for success in our everyday moments. Read Colossians 3:12-14 and list all the virtues we are to wear listing the "belt" last that ties the whole ensemble together. This accessories any outfit most perfectly on any occasion.

Let the king be enthralled by your beauty; honor him, for he is your lord. Psalm 45:11 (NIV)

WOW thank you for your tenacity this week dear one! May you be richly rewarded for your faithful pursuit of His heart with so much more of Him!

Please record the point of greatest impact from today.

Day 6 & 7: A Time To Reflect

Over the next two days take time to reflect over your week of study. Maybe you need some time to catch up on the study material and this might be the perfect break to do just that with the Lord!

I encourage you to glance back at the final point at the end of each day that you recorded having had the greatest impact on your heart. As you spend time with God in prayer, reflect and record on the lines below how God is tying it all together and applying it to your life.

Ask that God make it clear who He would have you invite into a natural opportunity to share Him, to apply what you are learning. Trust Him to continue to take the lead. May we have a heart ever ready with eyes and ears out to the opportunities God wants to invite us into for His glory and praise.

Do not merely listen to the word, and so deceive yourselves. Do what it says. Anyone who listens to the word but does not do what it says is like someone who looks at his face in a mirror and, after looking at himself, goes away and immediately forgets what he looks like. But whoever looks intently into the perfect law that gives freedom, and continues in it - not forgetting what they have heard, but doing it - they will be blessed in what they do. James 1:22-25 (NIV)

_____

_____

_____

_____

_____

Philippians 4:13 (NIV) *I can do all things through him who gives me strength.*

John 14:26 (NIV) *But the Advocate, the Holy Spirit, whom the Father will send in my name, will teach you all things and will remind you of everything I have said to you.*

WEEK 3

Whoever has ears, let then hear what the Spirit says to the churches. To the one who is victorious, I will give some of the hidden manna. I will also give that person a white stone with a new name written on it, known only to the one who receives it. Revelation 2:17 (NIV)

Day 1: LIVING Hope

Welcome sweet friend! Early this morning I saw what truly could possibly have qualified as a stunt double for the burning bush in Exodus 3:2! You know Moses was 80 years old when he was commissioned at the burning bush to save God's people. Between his advanced age, his murderous background and his lack of confidence in public speaking Moses could have figured social distance was going to be his life's way til death BUT God saw an amber in Moses' heart He could stoke for His glory!

God saw a guy with a spark of enthusiasm and curiosity at what He could do with a bush… though burning not burned up!?!! God saw a guy willing to draw near to His flaming strength in spite of his ghastly weaknesses! God saw a man, made not for distant aimless wanderings but for divinely designed deliverance!

Our Jesus is Living Hope and He still looks to use ambers within hearts. May today we ask for eyes to see through whatever distance or distractions that may cover our minds in order to see His ever moving heart of deliverance! It will all be worth it dear one! You are worth it, thank you for joining me today.

After beginning in prayer please join me in Matthew 22:23-33 _____, Mark 12:18-27 _____, and Luke 20:27-40. _____

So after the Pharisees trap failed regarding taxes, the Sadducees move to another topic to try and trip Jesus up; the afterlife.

In Mark 12:24 what does Jesus say their mistake is?

_____

Not knowing Scripture and not knowing the power of God.

Could that be our problem too in some situation or area of our lives? Are we focusing on all that we don't know instead of spending time pouring over all that we do, or at least should know… His Word and His unmatched power?!! Let's pray today to focus on our higher reality and take up joy in Truth we know stands eternally!

Take a moment to reflect and record. What do you know from Scripture and about the death defying power of God that can be applied to bring peace to our minds and hearts within a situation of which you are unsure about? (If you have been traveling this journey since book one you may want to look back over the notes you have gathered from His Word so far in each book.) We all have the big book, the Bible, so go back to what you know is rock solid Truth like, Psalm 27:1 (NIV) *The LORD is my light and my salvation-- whom shall I fear? The LORD is the stronghold of my life-- of whom shall I be afraid?* Truth like Psalm 23 and John 14:1-3…

Again, think for a moment and record at least one Truth that you know is solid from His Word. A Truth that you can trust and stand up steady on.

_____
_____
_____
_____

Maybe find a sticky note and designate one wall or spot in your house that you can start posting these Truths. That way when you hit a wall, (so to speak) and we all do in this world, it won't take us down but will rather redirect us to our wall of Truth that will steady and encourage and build us up so that we can keep going! *You, LORD, keep my lamp burning; my God turns my darkness into light. With your help I can advance against a troop; with my God I can scale a wall.* Psalm 18:28-29 (NIV)

Jesus goes on to explain in Mark 12:25 that the old order of things will be gone He will be doing something entirely new!! See Revelation 21:4-5. How does this encourage you that nothing will be a disappointment for those in Jesus, come eternity?!! Before responding below please read Isaiah 64:4 and 1 Corinthians 2:9 which confirm and stir our hearts with anticipation in what is to come!!

_____

_____

What event in Scripture does Jesus point to in Mark 12:26?

_____

At the burning bush who does God tell Moses He is? And what can we glean from the afterlife through what God claims about Himself?

_____

_____

He is a God of the living not the dead!!! (Mark 12:27) Let's not let our discouraging moments or seasons let us lose sight of this Truth! We do not want to make such a serious error! Our God is LIVING HOPE! The kind that does not disappoint! (Rom. 5:5) It will be so worth it dear one!! 2 Corinthians 4:17 (NIV) *For our light and momentary troubles are achieving for us an eternal glory that far outweighs them all.* The glory will be so great our troubles now will seem light and momentary!!!!! WOW!

Praise be to the God and Father of our Lord Jesus Christ! In his great mercy he has given us new birth into a living hope through the resurrection of Jesus Christ from the dead, 1 Peter 1:3 (NIV)

Let's stop and rest here for the day, right in the lap of Living Hope dear one. *Therefore, there is now now condemnation for those who are in Christ Jesus,* Romans 8:1 (NIV) Please record what had the greatest impact on your heart today while you studied His Word.

_____

_____

_____

_____

Day 2: Set Your Focus

Welcome back friend! I hope you are alive with Hope and hungry for the sustenance that only our Bread of Life can offer. *Then Jesus declared, "I am the bread of life. Whoever comes to me will never go hungry, and whoever believes in me will never be thirsty.* John 6:35 (NIV) *Satisfy us in the morning with your unfailing love, that we may sing for joy and be glad all our days.* Psalm 90:14 (NIV) Please bow in prayer before God Almighty, honoring His leadership, asking that He make our hearts ever more soft and receptive to His will, way and timing.

Traveling on now to Matthew 22:34-40 _____ and Mark 12:28-34. _____

I tell you what, if there is anyone who understands the daily grind it's Jesus! If it wasn't the Sadducees it was the Pharisees and if not the Pharisees it was the

Sadducees going at Him time and time again in effort to trip Him up! Here we see the Pharisees again step into the ring of antagonism!

Nehemiah, in the book of Nehemiah, is working at rebuilding the wall around Jerusalem and is constantly under the ridicule of mean men trying to distract and ultimately defeat his great work and purpose. The enemy doesn't need to defeat us to render us ineffective for God's Kingdom, he needs only to keep us distracted from His calling on our lives. Dear one where is your focus today?

Please read Nehemiah 6:2-3 and record your own declaration of correctly placed and determined focus for today!

_____

_____

Now list the first and second greatest commandments as depicted by Jesus Himself in Mark 12:30-31. Let this be your focus today.

_____

_____

_____

_____

List practical ways you can live these verses out today.
Love God with all your heart:

_____

Love God with all your soul:

_____

Love God with all your mind:

_____

Love God with all your strength:

_____

Love others as yourself:

_____

Mark 12:34 indicates the man who knew these commands was close to entering the Kingdom of God. It is not enough to know the commands but by faith, obediently following them is what truly matters. Let's not stop at close but let's go all the way in! It will be well worth it, so let's set our focus on Jesus and move in the only direction faith faces, forward!

Therefore, since we are surrounded by such a great cloud of witnesses, let us throw off everything that hinders and the sin that so easily entangles. And let us run with perseverance the race marked out for us, fixing our eyes on Jesus, the pioneer and perfecter faith. For the joy set before him he endured the cross, scoring its shame, and sat down at the right hand of the throne of God. Hebrews 12:1-2 (NIV)

Thank you dear one! See you back here tomorrow but first record what impacted your heart and mind most from your study of His Word today.

_____

_____

_____

_____

Day 3: Hilariously Giving

Hi! I'm trusting God to faithfully take the lead and lead our hearts deeper into His as we humbly lay them before His throne. Please take a moment in prayer to acknowledge and reverence His leadership today before proceeding.

Please meet me on the other side of Matthew 22:41-46 _____, Mark 12:35-37 _____ and Luke 20:41-44. _____

We read how those who opposed Jesus asked questions in an attempt to trip Him up. Here we see Jesus turn the table and ask a question of His own. What question does He ask them in Matthew 22:42?

_____

The most important question we too will ever answer in our lives is, who do we say Jesus is?

Revelation 22:16 (NLT) states, *"I, Jesus, have sent my angel to give you this message for the churches. I am both the source of David and the heir to his throne. I am the bright morning star."*

As Creator God, He existed long before David but coming to earth in human form He was one of David's descendants. (See Isaiah 11:1-5)

For our last segment of Scripture today please turn and read Mark 12:41-44 _____ and Luke 21:1-4. _____

Jesus was in the part of the Temple known as the Court of Women. Jesus regularly taught there so that women could hear his teaching too. He was watching that day as people gave. God's eyes roam the earth to strengthen those who are fully devoted to Him, 2 Chronicles 16:9 tells us. He sees when we struggle with anxiety over making ends meet yet trying to be faithful in tithing; trusting His promise in Philippians 4:19 that He will supply all of our needs. He sees when we strive to be good stewards of the treasure He has given us and when we fall short to the temptation of our flesh. His eyes roam to strengthen and not to condemn. He knows the struggle money can put on a heart so He is there to strengthen us in this area of great human weakness.

Recall the encouragement of Malachi 3:10.

52

2 Corinthians 9:7 tells us God loves a cheerful giver. The word cheerful in Greek translates hilaros[2]. Could God be asking us to give with hilarious generosity because He is the Source that replenishes and He never runs out!?!! Do we give cheerfully? Do we give hilariously? Does God have an area He might want to stretch our faith, grow our faith, by stepping out a bit further in this area?

_____

_____

This woman gave freely, willingly. How many coins did she give according to Luke 21:2?

_____

Two small coins. It doesn't seem like much but when it's all you have it's a whole lot. God doesn't look at the amount given as much as the condition of the heart behind what is given. He can feed thousands with five loaves and two fish, He is not in need of our resources. He longs to set us free! Free from all sorts of things such as the bondage of greed, worry and self-reliance which is only a false sense of security anyway! Free to abide in the Source of all resources! He never runs dry and knows the details of our need before we do and loves us beyond our comprehension.

Trusting when we can't see the provision is not easy. How can you find Him faithful if you never step out into a situation that requires Him to show Himself as such?

In God's world 5 loaves + 2 fish = 5,000 remainder 12!!

---

[2] G2431 - hilaros - Strong's Greek Lexicon (KJV). Retrieved from https://www.blueletterbible.org//lang/lexicon/lexicon.cfm?Strongs=G2431&t=KJV

2 Corinthians 8:2 (NIV) states, *In the midst of a very severe trial, their overflowing joy and their extreme poverty welled up in rich generosity.*

WHAT?! Only in God Almighty can severe trial and extreme poverty be found in the same sentence to equal overflowing joy and rich generosity!

Stay the course, keep the faith, follow through… it will all be worth it dear one, well worth it.

For you know the grace of our Lord Jesus Christ, that though he was rich, yet for your sake he became poor, so that you through his poverty might become rich. 2 Corinthians 8:9 (NIV)

Please record the point of greatest impact from today.

_____

_____

_____

_____

Day 4: Keep Watch For Him

I say to you what I say to everyone: Watch for him!" Mark 13:37 (NLT)

Today I was out on a trail behind my home and wouldn't you know God brought me to school and I didn't even know there was class! Praise that He needs no walls or schedule to show up and meet with His kids! All the world is His classroom and all time is in His Almighty hand!

So today my path was hidden in the thickest of fog. I was literally walking inside a cloud and have you ever felt like your literal life path seems to be following that same unseen path within a foggy cloud of uncertainty?! We can only praise The certain One, that promises to be all that He has said He is in His faithful Word through all that we go through. He will never leave us alone.

As I walked I was reminded that when the path seems so unclear I need to relinquish the weight I was never conditioned to carry called, the illusion of control. Why sweat buckets over trying to figure it all out when clearly God is working it all out! (Romans 8:28)

Sometimes God's provision comes in the form of a project so that I learn the dance of dependence. Oh what a dence (dance) that is to learn for those of us that like to carry the illusion of control! The instructions are rarely found "in the box" but rather in His hand.

Just because we can't see the way does not mean we are not equipped to dance this way… it does mean it will be by way of trust and dependence on Him who does see, hear and know, and is The Way.

Let's bow in prayer to honor His leadership as we begin to "dance" this day in dependence on Him.

Please savor these passages regarding our future found in Matthew 24:1-51 _____, Mark 13:1-37 _____ and Luke 21:5-38. _____

Matthew 24 begins with Jesus talking about the destruction of the Temple. This structure was magnificent and so Jesus' words were hard to believe, hard to receive and even imagine. Just because we can't make sense of something God has decreed doesn't mean it's not true or won't come to pass. If He has said it, it will be.

...What I have said, that I will bring about; what I have planned, that I will do. Isaiah 46:11 (NIV)

Do you have a particular area in your life you feel God has given you His Word yet you are having to take it one step at a time by way of trust and not sight?

_____

Those who look to him for help will be radiant with joy; no shadow of shame will darken their faces. Psalm 34:5 (NLT)

Now in Matthew 24:3 we see the disciples wondering when... and what... around an event concerning Jesus. I'm sure we can all relate on some level right! Isaiah 55:8-9 reminds us His ways are so far beyond ours. We are often going to wonder when and what, when it comes to our God but thankfully Who is something we can know for certain without a shadow of a doubt by His Word. *Jesus Christ is the same yesterday and today and forever.* Hebrews 13:8 (NIV)

God declares His ways to be higher than ours (Is. 55:8-9). So might we stop fighting Him for the lower way just because it's what we can figure out?! Let's pray for increasing trust and faith to allow Him to blow our minds with His higher and better way as we walk with Him in obedience.

Where do we see Jesus located in verse 3?

_____

Mount of Olives. What does Zechariah 14:4-5 tell us about this location?

_____

_____

With one foot on either side of the Mount of Olives it splits right down the middle as an escape route for His people in these end times! Good golly talk about outside the box thinking! We need an escape route and God Almighty just splits our mountain of a trial right down the middle by standing on top of it!! What can stand against you when the one who stands with you is God Almighty!!!?!

What event were the disciples wondering about in Matthew 24:3?

_____

Jesus did not respond with a date and time but He does give us all signs to read the times. Why do you think Jesus would do this instead of giving a direct and specific time and day for His return?

_____

He wants the best for us and wants us to be ready. If He gave us a day and time we may get lax and begin living for self thinking we have time to clean up our act before God returns! He knows the strength of the enemy alongside that of our weakness in the flesh so to have given us a specific time really wasn't best for us. Requiring us to read the times beckons our focus to remain on Him so that the enemy cannot distract us from our higher calling and heavenly home! Consistently living God's way leads to being prepared for anything.

I wonder if when we seek Him for an answer in prayer asking God if we should choose a or b, or go left or right and we just don't seem to hear a clear answer, could it be He is wanting us rather to apply the wisdom He has already generously given us through His Word, to the situation in question?!

Going to Him continually in a love relationship in which His wisdom is given consistently and lavishly for any decision we may come up against, requires much more dependence on Him than simply seeking an a or b answer from Him. A dependence that nurtures a love relationship. If we seek Him continually for Him, rather than seek Him intermittently for some "thing", we just might find we already have all we need to know the way (a or b, left or right) in our "thing".

Back to Matthew 24:4-12. What are some of the signs and warnings Jesus gives?

_____

_____

_____

What does 2 Timothy 4:3 warn us of?

_____

_____

Know Truth so well that when counterfeit comes we spy it right off the bat! This takes intentional and continuous focus on the Truth within the Light. Since you have made it this far in such an in-depth study of His Word I can only assume you are already taking great lengths to be intentionally studying His heart of pure Truth and encouraging others to do the same.

I appreciate that verse 13 in Matthew 24 begins with "but" (NIV)! In all the horrific things that will prove the end of times is near, what is the "but" we get to rest in as believers in Jesus according to verse 13?

_____

Not only that but there is a wonderful "and" (NIV) that kicks off verse 14! What is the "and" leading to in verse 14?

_____

Endurance through the tough times leads to being saved AND in spite of hardship the Good News will still reach to the ends of the earth!

For which I am suffering even to the point of being chained like a criminal. But God's word is not chained. 2 Timothy 2:9 (NIV)

I enjoy the parenthesis found in Matthew 24:15 (NKJV) which states, *(whoever reads, let him understand),* Oh what a prayer to insert everywhere I read His Word!!

There is such urgency for us all in this message regarding the end of times. There is no pause button on the Kingdom calendar. Living ready not only benefits us but also others as they see the contrast you live out in the world. The world will take notice and wonder… what are you ready for?! Thus is our opportunity to share Jesus, the One coming back for us!

Please record Matthew 24:25 below.

_____

He is always with us and there is nothing He doesn't already know or have the strength for us to face as He has overcome this world. We have His Word on this already! How does knowing this beforehand, before our days, moments, situations and schedules, bring your heart a peace that passes understanding?

_____

John 16:33 (NIV) *"I have told you these things, so that in me you may have peace. In this world you will have trouble. But take heart! I have overcome the world."*

Matthew 24:30 indicates what emotion will be experienced among the peoples of the earth?

_____

There will be great mourning for those that have chosen to reject Jesus and realize when it's too late that they have chosen the wrong side. This will break God's heart too but He honors our choice. Remember 2 Peter 3:9.

In Matthew 24:32 He gives us a warning lesson through what illustration?

_____

A fig tree. In verse 37 He gives us another warning lesson through what Bible story from the Old Testament?

_____

Noah and the Ark. Mark 13:34-37 gives yet another story illustration. Briefly record it below.

_____

Matthew 24:35 warns us what will never pass away?

_____

HIS WORDS!! It is the one sure foundation we have to stand on! Jesus is the Word of Truth! (John 14:6, John 1:1)

Do you hear the urgency of God's warning to all humanity?! The point is not to figure out the day and time of His second coming but to live in such a way of wholehearted devotion to Him that magnifies Truth, His Word and Way so that not only will we be found ready and prepared for His return but others will be made known of His great love for them too. Living ready for a loving Fathers return holds no fear, for perfect love casts out fear (1 John 4:18). Mark 13:9 gives us warning that we too will experience persecution BUT this is an opportunity to what?!

_____

Be a witness for Christ! What sure hope of encouragement follows in verse 11?

_____

And why? See verse 10.

_____

In all the trials God is on the move for good! This has been God's way from the beginning!! The first book of the Bible records, Genesis 50:20 (NIV) *You intended to harm me, but God intended it for good to accomplish what is now being done, the saving of many lives.*

Acts 23:6, 11 records Paul on trial for having the hope of the resurrection of the dead however, (verse 11 NIV) *The following night the Lord stood near Paul and said, "Take courage!…* God stood by Paul and was Paul's faithful source of encouragement! 2 Timothy 4:16-18 (NIV) records Paul saying, *At my first defense, no one came to my support, but everyone deserted me. May it not be held against them. But the Lord stood at my side and gave me strength, so that through me the message might be fully proclaimed and all the Gentiles might hear it. And I was delivered from the lion's mouth. The Lord will rescue me from every evil attack and will bring me safely to his heavenly kingdom. To him be glory for ever and ever. Amen.*

God shows no favoritism, He is the same always (Rom. 2:11, Heb. 13:8). God shows up for His people. He will show up for you in the way He knows is best and we can almost certainly count on it being in an Ephesians 3:20 kind of way! Way beyond how we would have expected but that is just what keeps the romance alive is it not!!?! Our biggest thrill, our grandest adventure will always, always be Jesus!! Praise His victorious name!

In any time, all the time, God is good and He is with you. Make known this love through the readiness by which you live.

This is our opportunity!

Luke 21:34 (NLT) *"Watch out! Don't let your hearts be dulled by carousing and drunkenness, and by the worries of this life. Don't let that day catch you unaware,*

Luke 21:19 (NLT) *By standing firm, you will win your souls.*

Thank you for your extreme diligence and tenacity in study. Please record the point of greatest impact on your heart today.

_____

_____

_____

_____

Day 5: Dance, Dance, Dance!

Hi! I want to share Zechariah 2:5 (ESV) as we begin today, *And I will be to her a wall of fire all around, declares the LORD, and I will be the glory in her midst.'"*

Oh that He would feel welcome in the midst of our study today and be the glory, the wonder and awe within our hearts! Please pray with me that we get out of His way so that He can lead us deeper into Him on the dance floor of life.

Today we will walk through the first of three parables of which Jesus continues to express the urgency and importance of living ready and prepared for His return. The first parable teaches us that our spiritual condition is our responsibility. The second parable will show us the importance of being a good steward of the gifts God has entrusted to us. Thirdly we will read on the importance of caring for those in need.

Please meet me on the other side of Matthew 25:1-13. _____

In verse 2 what is the ratio of foolish bridesmaids to wise ones?

_____

So could there be a fifty fifty chance we would find ourselves in the group we don't want to be in?! I mean that seems pretty risky considering eternity is what hangs in the balance!

Please read 1 Corinthians 10:12. This warning is issued to who?

_____

Those who THINK there are standing FIRMLY! This warning is not for those teetering on the edge or toying with fire or walking the line of shady indifference. No, this warning is for those that totally think they are firmly in the wise 50%. Why would you need a warning if where you think you are residing in thought, word and action is in the wise 50%?

_____

Because maybe where we THINK we are, is not where we are in reality.

So how do we heed a warning if we don't think we need it? Well, because the Word has given it we need to heed it. We need to ask God to evaluate what we are using as measuring sticks for our lives. The world's measuring sticks are constantly in a state of flux. Just look at the various fads throughout the decades to see clear evidence of that. One day you need this haircut and these shoes and your jeans need to be tight rolled at the bottom just so, to be "cool"! However next week you better not be caught dead with jeans tight rolled because that is "so yesterday"! The Word of God is flawless and He is unchanging says Proverbs 30:5 and Malachi 3:6 so that is where we should derive our unchanging standard for living.

Jeremiah 17:10 tells us the Lord searches all hearts and examines secret motives. It's a good thing too as some motives may be secret even to us! One verse back, Jeremiah 17:9 tells us the heart is deceitful above all else.

So we pray for God to search us and reveal to us where we stand in reality and that He gives us grace to embrace an obedient attitude of humility toward Him.

Psalm 139:23-24 (NIV) *Search me, God, and know my heart; test me and know my anxious thoughts. See if there is any offense way in me, and lead me in the way everlasting.*

In Matthew 25:3-4 what was the deciding factor that placed each bridesmaid in either the wise or foolish category?

_____

Responsibility. They all knew where they were going and what was needed. Some did not prepare with an attitude of reverence or holy fear for the occasion they were attending. Would a bride forget to wear her wedding gown to her wedding?! No, it's too important. How important is our belief in the flawless Word of God?

Verse 5 indicates ALL the bridesmaids did what?

_____

Fell asleep. We all are going to fall short, there will be times we "fall asleep" but it is the one that continually wakes up to their shortcoming and fall's back down at the Father's feet pleading the blood of the Lamb shed to restore and redeem us, to wake us up to the new life He died to give us, asking forgiveness, receiving restoration in humility. That bridesmaid "wakes up" realizes she was made for more and picks back up that sacred Light of Him in her and again watches in readiness prepared for His return.

Proverbs 24:16 (NIV) *for though the righteous fall seven times, they rise again, but the wicked stumble when calamity strikes.*

Matthew 25:13 (NLT) *"So you, too, must keep watch! For you do not know the day or hour of my return.* A warning doesn't get more personal! We must keep watch because we do not know! We do not know it all but we know the One who does so we must treasure and trust His flawless Word today. We must heed it's instructions today, right now this very moment!! Tomorrow, tonight, might be too late!

Turn Psalm 139:23-24 into a prayer, asking that He search our heart and that we are receptive to His flawless evaluation. No matter how firmly we think we are standing let Him be the judge and if He says we need to shift our stance, oh dear one, let's not stand in debate but heed His instruction so we don't find ourselves caught without oil in the night!

Let's meet over our next parable found in Matthew 25:14-30. _____

Depending on your version of the Bible verse 14 may indicate the man was going on a long journey or to a far country. The idea is that it would be some time before he returned thus a parallel in the time it may seem like before Jesus second coming.

There are different amounts entrusted to different servants. To the first servant how much silver was entrusted?

_____

To the second servant how much was entrusted?

_____

How much silver was entrusted to the third servant?

_____

Although they were all given different amounts of silver to steward they all had the same job title. What was it?

Servant. Regardless of the amount they had been entrusted with, they still all held the same title, the same position, they held the same worth. Each was just a servant. The amount they had been entrusted with did not make one more valuable than the other. How might you take this thought and apply it to the way you view yourself and others in light of the different gifts, talents, abilities and doors of opportunity each has been given?

The talent you have been entrusted with does not determine your personal worth or value. All humans were made for one purpose, we have one title: servants of the King of kings and Lord of lords. God shows no favoritism.

He has given His servants different tasks and His concern is over obedience to that which He has asked of you. God, the Author of all time does not waste it. If He has asked you to complete a task it's because in His mind (which is far greater than ours) He has good reason to see the task completed, not to have our opinion on whether we feel it's worthy of completion. If He assigned it, it has value.

I find myself at yet another "dance" I need to learn. Obedience. Anyone know of a dance school that teaches both the Obe-"dience" dance and the Depen-"dence" on Him, dance?! Oh ya, those dance instructions are found in the Bible and usually put to the music of praise!

According to verse 19 in Matthew 25 when did the master return?

After a looooooong time. So we are back to the patient endurance thing... Oh good golly, another dance! En-"durance" dance!

Dance, dance, dance! Obedience, dependance, endurance! The dance floor would be pretty empty if only the best got out there!

Matthew 25:25 tells us why the servant with one talent hid his. Why did he do so?

_____

Fear. What has kept you off the dance floor of life?

_____

We don't want our God to return to find us sitting on the bench with our dancing shoes still in pristine condition. No! I want hole's in my soles! I want the rug to be on fire with clothes drenched through with sweat so when He cuts in I can look into His eyes with God-confidence (God-confi-"dence", another "dance" you only learn dancing with Him!) and say, "I used every bit of talent You gave me, I have nothing left."

Friend, you were made to dance! Let's dance for Him, an audience of One.

Matthew 25:29-30 (NLT) ...*But from those who do nothing… Now throw this useless servant into outer darkness, where there will be weeping and gnashing of teeth.'*

Choosing to sit on the sidelines, to do nothing, for any reason when God has given you a beat to dance to within the gift of your own heart is to be useless! And what a crime for 1 Corinthians 15:58 tells us NOTHING we would choose to do for God is useless! Praise God He can use even my dance steps!

If we step out into His will with a trusting faith, eyes solely on His, as Judge, rather than on humans, then all we'll see is His approving smile. We won't be worried about the skill of our soles because our soul that counts won't be stepping but dancing in time with the life sustaining, all sufficient beat of His heart.

Please dance with me over to Matthew 25:31-46. _____

What two animals are depicted in this segment of Scripture?

_____

Just like the prepared and unprepared bridesmaids we have the believers (sheep) and the unbelievers (goats) that all travel together until the end of the line. There will be an end of the line for all of us and then Truth will be told.

What acts qualified a sheep (verses 34-36)?

_____

_____

Acts of service are not sustained by our love for Christ but rather His love for us. To begin to know by faith this love that surpasses knowledge we can't help but see it result in action. Actions from an overflowing fountain of love being received into our heart from Christ. It's a natural power of will He works in us to accomplish every good thing that pleases Him. Hebrews 13:20-21 (NIV) *Now may the God of peace, who through the blood of the eternal covenant brought back from the dead our Lord Jesus, that great Shepherd of the sheep, equip you with everything good for doing his will, and may he work in us what is pleasing to him, through Jesus Christ, to whom be glory for ever and ever. Amen.*

Take a moment and list practical ways you can be intentional about meeting the needs of those God has placed in your sphere of influence. (Isaiah 58, Ezekiel 18:7 and James 1:26-27 also offer some good advice on this topic.)

_____

_____

Proceed in prayer as God knows best how to reach the depths of the individual hearts He Himself has knit intricately together. God Almighty must lead.

Life in Christ is a partner dance. You and Jesus. You never walk on the dance floor alone and God must always lead. He's your floor, your music, your rhythm, your stamina, confidence… He is the choreographer of the dance. Remain in Him.

To him who is able to keep you from stumbling and to present you before his glorious presence without fault and with great joy-- Jude 1:24 (NIV)

Dance, dance, dance with God - just follow His lead!
Please record the point of greatest impact from today.

_____

_____

_____

_____

Day 6 & 7: A Time To Reflect

Over the next two days take time to reflect over your week of study. Maybe you need some time to catch up on the study material and this might be the perfect break to do just that with the Lord!

I encourage you to glance back at the final point at the end of each day that you recorded having had the greatest impact on your heart. As you spend time with God in prayer, reflect and record on the lines below how God is tying it all together and applying it to your life.

Ask that God make it clear who He would have you invite into a natural opportunity to share Him, to apply what you are learning. Trust Him to continue to take the lead. May we have a heart ever ready with eyes and ears out to the opportunities God wants to invite us into for His glory and praise.

Do not merely listen to the word, and so deceive yourselves. Do what it says. Anyone who listens to the word but does not do what it says is like someone who looks at his face in a mirror and, after looking at himself, goes away and immediately forgets what he looks like. But whoever looks intently into the perfect law that gives freedom, and continues in it - not forgetting what they have heard, but doing it - they will be blessed in what they do. James 1:22-25 (NIV)

_____

_____

_____

_____

_____

Philippians 4:13 (NIV) *I can do all things through him who gives me strength.*

John 14:26 (NIV) *But the Advocate, the Holy Spirit, whom the Father will send in my name, will teach you all things and will remind you of everything I have said to you.*

WEEK 4

To the one who is victorious and does my will to the end, I will give authority over the nations — Revelation 2:26 (NIV)

Day 1: You Find What You Look For

Hello, welcome to study my friend. Yesterday my daughter was baptized!! All of heaven erupted in joy as did our hearts! She was baptized in a lake near our home and in the water she picked up a stone in the shape of a heart. Jesus is the Rock of her heart and has given her eyes to perceive His love notes to her all around!

What you look for you will find. I've heard it stated, if you really want to find a way you will find one, if not, you will find an excuse. Praying daily for eyes and ears to perceive His ever moving presence and then a heart willing to fall instep alongside Him in this dance called life. I pray to dance in obedience, dependence and patient endurance all the way till the music stops and a new song begins on the other side of heaven when we will all get a new pair of dancing shoes! So let's dance this one out until our soles wear through, shall we!!?!

Please open in prayer asking that we follow His lead before beginning.

Please meet me in Matthew 26:1-5 _____, Mark 14:1-2, _____ and Luke 22:1-2. _____

In Matthew 26:2 What does Jesus say the disciples know?

_____

Jesus states, *"As you know…"* (NLT) and goes on to remind the disciples that in two days it would be Passover.

Passover was an event one would not miss. All Jewish males over the age of 12 from all over the Roman world were required to go to Jerusalem for the Passover celebration which would then be followed by the seven day Festival of Unleavened Bread. Jerusalem at this time would have been busting at the seams with travelers from all over!

Jesus knew His disciples were about to enter into a time that would rock their world, sending their minds reeling to say the least, so in preparation He takes them back to what they know and are sure of. Jesus begins, "As you know…" in two days it will be Passover. They knew Passover was a time to remember back and celebrate the faithfulness of their God. Back in Exodus 12 God used the sacrificial blood of a lamb to save their lives; death passed over them.

The Festival of Unleavened Bread reminds the Israelites of God's quick rescue and their immediate escape from Egypt, so quick in fact that they did not have time for their bread to rise so they baked it without yeast (unleavened).

Remember in our study, Jesus warned the disciples of the yeast or sin of the Pharisees back in Matthew 16:6. Jesus is the sinless Lamb of God whose blood would be poured out to save our lives that death might pass over those of us who believe. Jesus is the pure Bread of life. *So if the Son sets you free, you are truly free.* John 8:36 (NLT)

Jesus seems to be taking this moment to take His men back to what they knew was Truth to anchor them in all that they had yet to fully comprehend. What else did Jesus remind His men of in addition to the two days till Passover in Matthew 26:2?

_____

He would be crucified. He would be the Lamb slain to overcome our sin and save us all! Ultimately this was going to be for the good of the entire world!

According to Matthew 26:3 the chief priests and the elders of the people (the ones you would have expected to have been supportive of Jesus) were meeting together or rather scheming to do what according to verse 5?

_____

It's amazing how we will see God take what the people meant for harm and use it to bring about the biggest blessing mankind will ever know!

Have you ever experienced a negative that God brought about a bigger positive through, that you never would have imagined possible?

_____

"What do you mean, 'If I can'?" Jesus asked. "Anything is possible if a person believes." Mark 9:23 (NLT)

Moving forward please read, Matthew 26:14-16 _____, Mark 14:10-11 _____ and Luke 22:3-6. _____

In Luke 22:3 what happened?

_____

Remember back in Luke 4 when Satan had previously tempted Jesus… what does Luke 4:13 tell us?

_____

He left Jesus until an opportune time. It seems Satan found his opportune time through Judas, one of Jesus 12 disciples.

1 Peter 5:8 (NIV) tells us, *Be alert and of sober mind. Your enemy the devil prowls around like a roaring lion looking for someone to devour.*

We can't say exactly what door Judas opened for the devil to enter him but John 12:6 does tell us Judas was the thief that stole from the disciples community money. It seems money had become a trip hazard for Judas causing his heart and mind to stray from the one true God.

Jesus is the Lion of the Tribe of Judah. Revelation 5:5 (NIV) *Then one of the elders said to me, "Do not weep! See, the Lion of the tribe of Judah, the Root of David, has triumphed. He is able to open the scroll and its seven seals."*

Do you see that as Jesus is the Lamb that was slain He is also the Lion who has triumphed! Who does the devil masquerade around as?! The lion!! Satan plays the counterfeit lion, a lion that deceives and traps and kills! Dear one, we must keep watch! We must remain in the Light to know Truth so well we perceive counterfeit right off before he stays long enough to outwit us and sink his teeth into us!!

Maybe Judas suffered from unmet expectations in thinking Jesus was a military king? Maybe he was jealous of Peter, James and John that got pulled aside to be with Jesus often? Maybe he didn't understand and couldn't make sense of all that Jesus seemed to be doing so he had given up trying? What door are we leaving vulnerably open and available to the enemy in our own lives? Jesus already knows our hearts, might we just confess it all so that He might come in with His fortifying Truth and guard us against the enemies lies!! Please take a moment in prayer and speak anything He lays on your heart as you listen in return. Record anything below that you feel led to.

_____

_____

_____

_____

The leading priests were planning on waiting until after Passover but to their delight Judas had made it easy for them to proceed immediately. However do you see that God continued to use all things to proceed on HIS Kingdom calendar?! No plan of God's can be thwarted! So what was Judas on the lookout for according to Luke 22:6? An opportunity for what?

_____

An opportunity to betray Jesus. And you know what, he found one.

We will find what we look for. What are you looking for? What do you look for generally in your days? Do you look for the good in people, places and perspectives? Or do you look for problems?

Ask God to open your eyes and ears to perceive what He wants you to in all things then pray to receive and accept His perspective as He reveals it.

Matthew 13:16 (NIV) *But blessed are your eyes because they see, and your ears because they hear.*

Jeremiah 29:13 (NIV) *You will seek me and find me when you seek me with all your heart.*

What are you looking for dear one? I hope it's a spot on the dance floor with Jesus because I know He's got your name on His dance card.

Please turn with me to our final portion of scripture today in Matthew 26:17-19 _____, Mark 14:12-16 _____, and Luke 22:7-13. _____

Matthew 26:17 presents an interesting question for us all to ponder I think. Where should we prepare a meal for Him? Where has God asked you to in a sense prepare a meal for Him? Who has He placed in your sphere of influence to impact with His love? How are we preparing our hearts for the future banquet meal with Him in heaven? Take a moment to reflect with God on these questions. Record a response if you felt led below.

_____

_____

He is the Bread of Life. Every morning we get to wake up we can pray… Dear Lord, where would you like me to prepare a meal for You, the Bread of Life, to be received?

In Luke 22:10 it indicates the disciples would find a man carrying water in which they were to approach. This would have been odd or maybe rather easy to spot as it was usually the women not the men carrying water.

I wonder if that man had complained about having to carry the water that day? I wonder if he almost didn't because he would have been too embarrassed by the onlookers stares and smirks? I wonder if maybe he did it with joy, seeing it as an opportunity to serve, possibly his ill wife? I don't know, but what opportunity might we miss because we are too worried about what others would think or we refuse to humble ourselves to such a position?

I'm sure this man never forgot the day he had to carry the water! I'm sure his story quickly changed from HAVING to carry the water to, he GOT to carry the water that day, after Jesus came to eat at his house!!! What situation in our lives might we begin to see as we GET to do it rather than we HAVE to do it?

Remember opportunities and provision often come in the form of projects that teach the dance steps of dependence on Him.

Luke 22:12 (NLT) states, *He will take you upstairs to a large room that is already set up. That is where you should prepare our meal."*

Jesus directed His disciples to the guy who was willing to perform humble service, like carrying water through the streets; Jesus directed His disciples to the guy who was ready, who had a room already prepared for His presence. That guy got to host the Last Supper.

Dear one, keep watch for Him in heart, soul, mind and strength. Be ready to take the opportunity to get out on the dance floor and dance as God Almighty leads you in the choreography only He could have created… you will hear His music if it's His music you are looking for.

Keep watch, listen for His music... and dance!

Please record the point of greatest impact today.

_____

_____

_____

_____

Day 2: Beautiful Feet

Welcome, I'm just so glad you are here! Please begin in prayer and then please meet me on the other side of John 13:1-20. _____

In the first three verses what do we know about what Jesus knows and what He loves?

_____

He knew it was His time to leave this world, that the Father had given Him authority over everything and that He had come from God and would return to God. He loved the disciples during his ministry and now to the very end.

How do you think Jesus, who entered earth wrapped in human flesh as an infant, came to know so much about His divine purpose?

_____

In communion with His Heavenly Father. How do we come to know His specific purposes for our lives?

_____

In communion with our Heavenly Father. This is also where our love for others will grow. The more time we spend with the Father, in prayer and in His Word, the more we will find ourselves transforming into more of the image of His Son, Jesus.

As we read the Word, ask that the Father read you as you read Him. Ask that He stir up His Spirit within you as you read His heart. Pray that He reveals great and unsearchable things you do not know and that your faith and trust grow to receive it and live obedient to Him. May He be our life's deepest craving, biggest thrill and grandest adventure!

As we have studied Jesus' disciples along our way, we know a bit about their personalities and yet in spite of all their shortcomings it says in John 13:1 that He loved them not BY the end, but TO the end! He loved them from the start and all the way to the end. Dear one do you know He loves you right where you are and He will love you all the way to the end? Jesus loves you.

Interesting that after all that is stated in the first three verses about Jesus knowing He is from God Almighty and He has authority over everything that His response in verse 4 is to do what?!!

Get up and start serving!!! And not any kind of serving, what does Jesus get up and do for His disciples?

He washed their feet!! A job of a lowly slave.

If Jesus, God Himself, takes the posture of a slave and serves us in humility how much more are we to do the same as His followers? How can you practically live this out in thought, word and action?

Good intentions are just that, good, but follow through is where the blessing is at. May we follow Christ with some follow through.

In verse 6 what does Peter ask Jesus?

_____

Are you going to wash MY feet?! Do we regard the fact that His blood was shed to cleanse all parts of our lives reverently? Are we mindful of the things we watch on TV and listen to on the radio? Could it be we make allowances in the things we watch and listen to because we aren't actually "doing" it? Are some of the things we tolerate the very sins Jesus laid His life down for so that we might be cleansed of?!

Peter thought it would be crazy for Jesus to wash his feet, that was too lowly a job, Peter would not want Jesus stooping so low for him. But as Jesus told Peter, _"...Unless I wash you, you won't belong to me."_ John 13:8 (NLT)

Peter had yet to understand Jesus' example, that the greatest leaders are those who serve those they lead. What is the first and second greatest commandment (see Mark 12:30-31)?

_____

_____

What if your expression of love was through serving? The way we treat authority shows just who we give ultimate authority to in our lives. Do you work for a boss or The Boss?

Serving with all your heart, soul, mind and strength. How would your service to God and others look if you served in that way, always? Can you list specific things you do each day and how they might look different if you looked at it as an opportunity to serve God with all your heart, soul, mind and strength?

_____

_____

Jesus gave us His example to follow not just to know. Think about how our knowledge of His example is working itself out in our lives in such a way that an example for others to follow is being produced?

In John 13:10 why do you think Jesus said it was just the feet that needed washing if the whole body had been bathed?

_____

_____

Once you have chosen to accept Christ as Savior then you have been made new, washed clean. You don't need to continue accepting Jesus over and over (Ephesians 1:13-14, John 10:28). Although made new in Christ we are still human and will make mistakes, so a cleansing of our feet is necessary, so to speak, in that we want to walk in purity with our God. We must confess and ask forgiveness to be restored to an unencumbered relationship with Him via a "washing of our feet" through confession in prayer as often as needed.

Speaking of feet do you remember back to our first week of study when we talked about Asa the king of Judah who walked in the way of the Lord? If you need to you can glance back at week 1 day 3 for a quick refresher. 2 Chronicles 15:17 (NIV) tells us, … *Asa's heart was fully committed to the LORD all his life.* However I'm not sure how often Asa brought his feet back to be washed in God. I'm speaking figuratively however please read 2 Chronicles 16 ___ for an interesting story that involves Asa's feet in his last years.

What happened to Asa's feet?!! (See 2 Chronicles 16:12)

_____

According to this chapter what was Asa failing to do in his later years?

_____

Seek the Lord, rely on the Lord! He was placing his confidence in what he could see rather than take up faith in the God who gave him those eyes to see!

How can we ward off the infectious disease of thinking we know it all because we have been there, done that before? How can we be intentional in our effort to be humble before our all knowing God and take up the attitude of a continual learner?

_____

_____

"But blessed is the one who trusts in the LORD, whose confidence is in him. Jeremiah 17:7 (NIV) I don't want to miss a new thing God wants to do because I'm stuck in the old familiar way I know. *See, I am doing a new thing! Now it springs up; do you not perceive it? I am making a way in the wilderness and streams in the wasteland.* Isaiah 43:19 (NIV)

How beautiful on the mountains are the feet of those who bring good news, who proclaim peace, who bring good tidings, who proclaim salvation, who say to Zion "Your God reigns!" Isaiah 52:7 (NIV)

None of us want "diseased feet" especially when the Word tells us they can be beautiful! The key to beautiful feet is to walk with God, rely on God, when we wander into sin watch out that we don't stay there but rather walk back, no, run back and let Him wash us clean!

Now in John 13:18 the issue of Judas' betrayal becomes the topic for a third time (13:2,11). We can see this issue weighed on Jesus greatly. Jesus had chosen Judas yet Judas had embraced darkness rather than the Light.

The end part of verse 18 (NLT) states, ... *'The one who eats my food has turned against me.'* Now please look up Psalm 41:9.

None of this took Jesus by surprise, He knew the script, He had the Scriptures. What are we doing with the Scriptures?

Pleases record what made the most impact on your heart as you studied in His Word today.

_____

_____

_____

_____

Day 3: Remember Me

Hi! I'm so very grateful we never get a busy signal when we come before our God. We can always enter into communion with Him at any time. He's available 24/7 no matter what; no matter where we have been or what we have done we can always come in reverence to commune with Him. That is the beauty, that is the amazing grace of the cross.

Let us begin in communion with Him. Praying that He removes any and all distractions so our mind and heart can focus on His message; that we might be washed by His Word and leave saturated in Truth. May his name be honored and lifted high as we are encouraged in His presence.

Let's proceed now to Matthew 26:20-30 ____, Mark 14:17-26 ____, Luke 22:14-30 ____ and John 13:21-30. ____

In John 13:21 we see for a third time (also found in 11:33 in the story of Lazarus, and in the garden of Gethsemane in 12:27) Jesus is said to be very troubled. His love is so great that the loss and betrayal of just one is deeply troubling to Him. Remember this is the same God who would leave the 99 to find the one lost sheep. Judas refuses to be found and it breaks God's heart.

If you have someone over whom your heart breaks in prayer to come to a saving knowledge of Jesus, please remember the God who knit that soul together loves them even deeper than we could or can even fathom. God understands the depth of our hearts pain as we praying without ceasing for our loved ones to respond to the pursuit of God's love for them and all the world!

In John 13:26 Jesus identifies the one to betray Him. What is the signal?

_____

I wonder why Judas did not stop and question his actions especially after Matthew 26:25?! I wonder if Jesus has that same wonder about us though too at times. Maybe, like Judas, we can get so consumed with our own agenda that we get tunnel vision - a dangerous place to be wouldn't you say?!!

Jesus is never caught off guard. He is omniscient, or all knowing. Here in verse John 13:27 Jesus lets Judas know He knows and yet Judas, as verse 30 indicates, leaves at once to carry out his plan!! Tunnel vision. Satan definitely gets a foothold when he can get us to focus on me, myself and I.

Remember the parable we studied earlier on the ten bridesmaids... recall how we can slip into the wrong 50%. Satan is deceptive and the father of lies. Anytime he can draw our focus off God and onto self or anything else but the eternal Truth of God, it becomes a slippery slope toward the wayward 50%. Keep watch dear one, on God Almighty, in Him there is no darkness at all! Review 1 John 1:5 and Psalm 119:105.

It's easy to point fingers and judge Judas who made plans to betray Jesus and yet still came to the passover meal. But how different is it for us to proclaim Christ and have our lives live something opposite? We deny Him too when we don't trust Him. When we don't obey Him we reject His authority. Do our words, thoughts and actions match? Do we honor or deny Him by the way we live in all areas?

In Mark 14:22-23 what is the bread and wine of communion a symbol of?

_____

_____

Luke 22:19 (NLT) ...*Do this to remember me.*"

Please read 1 Corinthians 11:23-29. _____

What does 1 Corinthians 11:26 say we are proclaiming when we participate in the act of communion or taking the emblems of the bread and the wine (or juice served in most churches)?

_____

1 Corinthians 11:27 indicates this act is to be taken very seriously. To take communion in an unworthy manner, without first examining your heart and confessing any sin to Him, without coming before Him in humility, reverence and in gratitude for His great sacrifice makes us guilty of what (verse 27)?

_____

The celebration of communion must be done reverently as it humbles us before God. We confess sin and restate our need for Him as our Savior, our Guide. Communion reminds us we are forgiven, set free but it was costly, so costly we couldn't ever have paid the price. Jesus willingly stepped in on our behalf. We couldn't by heaven, couldn't earn heaven and we certainly do not deserve heaven. Communion encourages us to recommit our hearts, our lives to Him who is worthy of all our worship.

Jesus became the one time sacrifice for all sin. The sinless, spotless Lamb of God. See Hebrews 10:1-18 ____ and Hebrews 4:16. ____

What part of Romans 3:21-28 is most encouraging for you ?

_____

Justified by faith - period (verse 28). Jesus did it all, we need only believe to be saved. Romans 10:9 (NIV) *If you declare with your mouth, "Jesus is Lord," and believe in your heart that God raised him fro the dead, you will be saved.*

In Luke 22 after all this goes down what do the disciples decide should be the topic of discussion in verse 24?!

_____

They begin to argue about who of them will be greatest in the Kingdom?!!! And even still Jesus responds with astounding grace. The disciples did not even realize the depth of their offense and all that Jesus was doing at that very moment! It's again easy to point fingers at what seems so blatantly wrong with others. Could it be that the very things we notice so quickly to criticize in others is due to the fact that we too struggle in the same area in one way or another?! How else would we be able to identify it so quickly?!

Please record Matthew 7:5 below as we pray that God alerts us (only He knows how to get through our thick skulls at times) so that we don't find ourselves sitting in the wrong 50% short on oil the day He returns!

_____

_____

Please read 1 Peter 5:5-6. ____ It seems Peter eventually "got it" (we all need to humbly receive His washing) and by God's amazing grace He can help us "get it" too.

Please record what impacted your heart the most through your study today.

_____

_____

_____

_____

Day 4: Live To Worship

Hello friend. Today our passages of Scripture will run into our study tomorrow as well. After you pray go ahead and take your time reading through the following event recorded in all four gospels. Matthew 26:31-35 _____, Mark 14:27-31 _____, Luke 22:31-38 _____ and John 13:31-38. _____

Though these passages predict a major fall they are riddled with hope! According to Strong's Greek Lexicon (1680) the Greek word for hope is "elpis"[3]. Good golly that's pronounced el-pece! So the Greek word for hope is pronounced peace?! Really!?!! Only our God!

If we operate in the Truth of His Living Hope we will have His peace that passes understanding! The enemy would so like us to let go of His hope wouldn't he?!

Romans 15:13 (NIV) *May the God of hope fill you with all joy and peace as you trust in him, so that you may overflow with hope by the power of the Holy Spirit.*

Hebrews 9:14 (NLT) *Just think how much more the blood of Christ will purify our consciences from sinful deeds so that we can worship the living God. For by the power of the eternal Spirit, Christ offered himself to God as a perfect sacrifice for our sins.*

----

[3] G1680 - elpis - Strong's Greek Lexicon (KJV). Retrieved from https://www.blueletterbible.org//lang/lexicon/lexicon.cfm?Strongs=G1680&t=KJV

In that last verse it says we were freed from a guilty conscience, sinful deeds, why? So we could do what?

_____

Worship the living God!! Oh how the enemy would like to have us wallow in shame, regret and guilt, to be so weighed down we never feel like we can step forward in Him again! Ultimately this robs us of our true purpose and God Almighty of due worship! Jesus died to set us free from the enemies debilitating strongholds! Do not entangle yourself by believing the lies! Pray that God's Truth be the loudest reality in our hearts and minds!

...choose for yourselves this day whom you will serve,... Joshua 24:15 (NIV)

Matthew 26:31 (NLT) indicates Jesus had this discussion "on the way…" I don't know about you, but knowing what He knew, I might be reluctant to be "on my way…", especially alongside those who I knew would desert me!! Not Jesus, He walked with them, mission minded. What has taking a mission minded approach done for your willingness to proceed in the hard thing? Mission minded, meaning a focus on things above, not earthly things (Col.3:2) Or how might we approach things today with a mindset on His mission for our lives?

_____

How did Jesus know they would all turn their backs on Him? (Matt. 26:31)

_____

For the Scriptures say… AGAIN Jesus points us to the ultimate road map for life - the Scriptures!! Please look up Zechariah 13:7-9. ____

I will bring that group through the fire and make them pure. I will refine them like silver and purify them like gold. They will call on my name, and I will answer them. I will say,

'These are my people,' and they will say, 'The LORD is our God.'" Zechariah 13:9 (NLT)

God always has a remnant! Choose to be the remnant that is refined and purified by the trials, transformed more into His image rather than found bitter, rotting and left purely putrid by them.

How do we choose this beautifully refined remnant? I prayerful humble submission to His better way, one choice, one deep breath at a time dear one. We have to choose to let His promises trump our performance.

Matthew 26:31-32 relays that without even skipping a beat Jesus practically in the same breath as He walks along, relays He knows His companions will all desert Him in His death but afterward He will come find them and meet them where?

_____

Amazing right! He will be betrayed yet right here states He will also take the first step back toward them! Amazing grace!

Luke records the conversation in a beautiful way. Read Luke 22:31-32. ____
The last sentence in verse 32 in the NLT states it this way... *So when you have repented and turned to me again, strengthen your brothers.*

The denial of Peter and betrayal of Judas is not a whole lot different in that a sin is a sin. However the difference is what occurred afterward. Peter repented and turned toward Jesus - Judas sat in shame and guilt and committed suicide, outwitted by the enemy.

Jesus will not force any to turn to Him but remember the parable of the prodigal son? (Luke 15:11-32) The father RAN to his returning son!!!!

There is therefore now no condemnation for those who are in Christ Jesus. Romans 8:1 (ESV) NO condemnation!! When you see the word "therefore" you have to look for what it's there-for. So why is there no condemnation? Well, see Romans 8:2!! *For the law of the Spirit of life has set you free in Christ Jesus from the law of sin and death.*

Jesus has set you free to turn to Him, receive forgiveness, be washed white as snow and live to worship the God of no greater love and amazing grace!!!!

Do not gloat over me, my enemy! Though I have fallen, I will rise. Though I sit in darkness, the LORD will be my light. Micah 7:8 (NIV)

We are going to pick up again in these same Scriptures tomorrow but for now please record what God has impacted your heart with the most while you studied His Word of Truth today.

_____

_____

_____

_____

Day 5: Redeeming Love

Hi! I cannot wait to jump right in where we left off yesterday!! Please pray and review your Scriptures from this week's day 4 for context in todays final lesson of the week. Luke 24:45 (NIV) *Then he opened their minds so they could understand the Scriptures.*

Matthew 26:31-35 _____, Mark 14:27-31 _____, Luke 22:31-38 _____ and John 13:31-38. _____

Okay now with refreshed context please read 2 Corinthians 5:14-21. _____

What ministry has He given each of us? (verse 18-19)

_____

What does verse 20 tell us we are for Christ?

_____

We are His ambassadors so that Christ can make His appeal through us. Who's appeal? Christ's appeal! He is our source of reconciliation, it's His love, His forgiveness that we bring to others out of honor to the One who showed it to us first. As undeserving as we were, He reconciled us to Himself and now for His honor and glory we are to show His heart of reconciliation as He works what that looks like out through us on the lives of those around us.
Are you willing to be an ambassador of reconciliation for Christ who reconciled you to Himself? How might that look practically day to day in your sphere of influence?

_____

_____

What purpose does Jesus indicate He has for Peter upon repentance? (Luke 22:32)

_____

To strengthen others!

Please read 2 Corinthians 1:3-5. How has God enabled you to comfort and strengthen others?

_____

_____

Amos 9:9 (NLT) *"For I will give the command and will shake Israel along with the other nations as grain is shaken in a sieve, yet not one true kernel will be lost.*

In Luke 22:31 Jesus said Satan had asked to sift His disciples like what?

_____

Wheat. Satan was hoping to bring them all to spiritual ruin which is what he is after in our lives too!

Back in Deuteronomy 28:63-68 the judgment referred to in Amos was predicted. Israel turned away from God and Assyria would be allowed to invade and "sift like wheat". The nation would be purified through this invasion and captivity but God would not lose one true believer. Sinners do not get away and the believers will not be lost. For He is faithful and just.

Have you ever experienced a time of "sifting"? A time when you felt like things in your life were shaking out of control but in the end you recognized the need for certain things to be sifted out of your life so you could sit refined and surrounded by the unshakable Truth?

_____

_____

This process can be compared to "pruning" as defined in John 15:2 (NIV) *He cuts off every branch in me that bears no fruit, while every branch that does bear fruit he prunes so that it will be even more fruitful.* Let's never forget He disciplines the one he loves (Hebrews 12:6).

Luke 22:37 points us to another prophecy. What is it?

_____

He was counted among the transgressors or rebels.

Isaiah 53:12 (NLT) *I will give him the honors of a victorious soldier, because he exposed himself to death. He was counted among the rebels. He bore the sins of many and interceded for rebels.*

A rebel is not someone accidentally choosing wrong, a rebel is choosing to rebel against something; intentional sin. Jesus interceded, He stepped in for the accidental sin but also to save us from our sin of rebellion! He stepped in to show us grace even when we knew we were doing the wrong thing!!! That's amazing grace!! Too great a gift at too great a cost not to repent and turn to Him and receive the love and restoration He longs to lavish on each one of us rebels!!

Turn to Him dear one, there are those He would like you to strengthen as He strengths you. Don't let the enemy talk you out of your purpose, to worship and magnify the God of all comfort and mercies by LIVING the LIFE He died to give you in His OVERCOMING VICTORY!

In the gospel of John we see Jesus issuing a reminder. Knowing His time is short His last words of instruction were probably well thought out not wanting to waste one precious moment on the Kingdom calendar! John 13:33 (NLT) *Dear children, I will be with you only a little longer….* So what is this commandment Jesus issues in John 13:34?

_____

Love like Jesus.

In verse 35 what will this kind of love prove?

_____

That we His disciples.

When seeking true believers don't look for all the correctly checked boxes in their lives, look for the evidence of His love lived out practically moment by moment. Measure the love you see by His example set in His Word.

In John 13:36-37 Peter wants to know and do what?

_____

Peter wants to know the plan and go with! Jesus tells Peter he can't go with Him now but later Peter would follow Him. God had great plans for Peter just as He does for you and I. He knows the things that need to be sifted from our lives so that we can become stronger and more sturdy in Him; becoming more effective in our sphere of influence for Him.

Peter allowed Jesus to wash his feet. Our walk with God will require a constant and continual humbling before our God so that He can wash our feet, redeem and restore our walk and relationship with Him each time we wander.

Jesus rose from the grave conquering death, our greatest enemy. Remember His great sacrifice and you won't be able to forget how great His redeeming love for you is dear one.

Please record the point of greatest impact.

_____

_____

_____

_____

Day 6 & 7: A Time To Reflect

Over the next two days take time to reflect over your week of study. Maybe you need some time to catch up on the study material and this might be the perfect break to do just that with the Lord!

I encourage you to glance back at the final point at the end of each day that you recorded having had the greatest impact on your heart. As you spend time with God in prayer, reflect and record on the lines below how God is tying it all together and applying it to your life.

Ask that God make it clear who He would have you invite into a natural opportunity to share Him, to apply what you are learning. Trust Him to continue to take the lead. May we have a heart ever ready with eyes and ears out to the opportunities God wants to invite us into for His glory and praise.

Do not merely listen to the word, and so deceive yourselves. Do what it says. Anyone who listens to the word but does not do what it says is like someone who looks at his face in a mirror and, after looking at himself, goes away and immediately forgets what he looks like. But whoever looks intently into the perfect law that gives freedom, and continues in it - not forgetting what they have heard, but doing it - they will be blessed in what they do. James 1:22-25 (NIV)

_____

_____

_____

_____

_____

Philippians 4:13 (NIV) *I can do all things through him who gives me strength.*

John 14:26 (NIV) *But the Advocate, the Holy Spirit, whom the Father will send in my name, will teach you all things and will remind you of everything I have said to you.*

WEEK 5

The one who is victorious will, like them, be dressed in white. I will never blot out the name of that person from the book of life, but will acknowledge that name before my Father and his angels. Revelation 3:5 (NIV)

Day 1: The Gift

"Don't let your hearts be troubled. Trust in God, and trust also in me. John 14:1 (NLT)

Hello sweet friend, welcome back! Let's begin as we have much to study this week as we wade through farewells, prayer, agony, betrayal, trials and denial. Sounds like a risky wade I know but our Way is secure so we have nothing to fear. Let's begin in prayer praising Him whose grip is mighty enough to help and hold us up victorious in Him through it all. We will not be overtaken! Praise the One who has overcome!

Let's tuck this one into our hearts pocket for our journey. Psalm 63:8 (NLT) *I cling to you; your strong right hand holds me securely.*

Please meet me on the other side of John chapter 14 please. _____

Oh how you have to love a love note that opens with, *"Don't let your hearts be troubled...."* (John 14:1 NLT) right! We can all take a deep breath now! Do you see that little word "let" there in that first phrase? Please circle it.

"Let" indicates I have some control on the trouble my heart experiences. Let's choose NOT to let our hearts be troubled. His Truth must be our loudest reality, marinating in the fact that He is always with us and within us! We dwell with Him and He indwells us as believers in Jesus! Hallelujah!

We can tuck this verse of Truth in our hearts pocket today too which just might help us with not letting ourselves become troubled in this broken world: *The LORD himself goes before you and will be with you; he will never leave you nor forsake you. Do not be afraid; do not be discouraged."* Deuteronomy 31:8 (NIV)

Oh why not, here is one more! Let's just stuff our hearts pocket full of Truth treasures today!! *So do not fear, for I am with you; do not be dismayed, for I am your*

God. I will strengthen you and help you; I will uphold you with my righteous right hand. Isaiah 41:10 (NIV) AND … *"In repentance and rest is your salvation, in quietness and trust is your strength,…* Isaiah 30:15 (NIV)

In John 11:33, 12:27, 13:21 Jesus experienced being troubled yet He took confidence in His Father's limitless power. Record the three events that describe Jesus as troubled.

_____

_____

_____

The pain in our hearts over death.
Submitting to the Fathers will of the cross.
Betrayal of a friend.

Remember Hebrews 4:15 (NIV) *For we do not have a high priest who is unable to empathize with our weaknesses, but we have one who has been tempted in every way, just as we are -- yet he did not sin.*

Jesus knows what it's like to feel troubled and He overcame that emotion through trusting His good Heavenly Father. Here in John 14:1 Jesus is speaking from experience!! He says the way to overcome a troubled heart is to TRUST. Trust God! Trust His limitless power, eternal Truths and enduring love.

What does Jesus point to first to still our troubled hearts? (verse 2)

_____

There is enough room for you in His eternal Kingdom! Hebrews 12:2 tells us Jesus endured the cross for the joy set before Him! He persevered and endured by setting Himself on the promise ahead and that is just what He points us to in order to persevere under trial and trouble! Set yourself on the joy that lies ahead. We have Living Hope and a promise that is sure, guaranteed by His Spirit within us that there is room for us in His Kingdom of which He is coming for us! Let's pray for ever increasing trust in the One who has ALWAYS proven faithful to His Word!

We can rest in and trust these promises of God… He has a place for us… He will come get us… Eternity is promised to all who believe in Jesus! The details are unknown however we trust the One who has always proven faithful in every detail in the past as we choose to embark on this adventure forward, without troubled hearts!

Why? How? Because what does John 14:4 tell us?

_____

Jesus says, we know the way! To which Thomas exclaims, oh no Lord we do NOT know the way in fact we have no idea!!

Have you ever felt like Thomas?!

_____

1 John 3:20 tells us God is greater than our feelings! Jesus responds in John 14:6 with what reply?

_____

He Himself is the Way, Truth and Life! He is The Way-maker; trust Him.

John 14:12 (NLT) …*even greater works*… indicates, through the power of the Holy Spirit we can carrying the Good News of the gospel to the whole world!

John 14:13 tells us we can ask for anything in His name and He will do it. Asking for things that align with His will and hearts desire will guarantee positive results but still we must remain flexible in the way that outcome looks as we continue to be molded into His image to better perceive things from His perspective.

What proves our love for Jesus? (See John 14:15)

_____

Obedience.

What will the Father send according to John 14:16?

_____

What will He do for us according to verses 17 and 26?

_____

Guide us into all truth!! We know the Way and we have the Way in us and He's not going away!

What can we KNOW for certain as believers in Jesus according to John 14:20?

_____

How does Colossians 1:27 (below) back this up?

Colossians 1:27 (NLT) *For God wanted them to know that the riches and glory of Christ are for you Gentiles, too. And this is the secret: Christ lives in you. This gives you assurance of sharing his glory.*

The secret to an untroubled heart is knowing Christ and trusting He lives in you!!!!

How can you live this truth out practically so that others can see that you have a reality that reaches beyond this world and leaves you filled with hope and peace?

_____

2 Corinthians 1:20 reminds us that all God's promises are "yes" in Jesus! This verse also reminds us that our lives in Jesus should speak an "Amen" or "yes" to His glory! Do our lives portray a confident YES in the promises of God or do we live more of a troubled "I don't know"?!

John 14:17 tells us the world doesn't know Him because it's not looking for Him but to those that love Him, verse 21 tells us He reveals Himself! May we have senses tuned and alert to His presence, craving His love above all.

John 14:22 poses a good question, what is it?

_____

He has revealed Himself yet saves His deepest revelations for those that receive Him. Matthew 7:6 (NIV) tells us, *"Do not give dogs what is sacred; do not throw your pearls to pigs. If you do, they may trample them under their feet, and turn and tear you to pieces.*

We should follow His example. We can be a friend to all but we only become close friends with those we know will value and appreciate our friendship.

As this chapter closes Jesus urges us to REMEMBER what He has told us (verse 28). The enemy has no power over Him (verse 30) even though it would appear that way at the cross. Jesus trusted the Father who proved faithful and Jesus was raised victorious from the grave by the power of the Spirit, the same Spirit inside us as believers (Rom. 8:11)! Will we trust as Jesus did, not letting our hearts be troubled even when things do not appear to be succeeding? John 14:27 (NLT) tells us, *"I am leaving you with a gift - peace of mind and heart. And the peace I give is a gift the world cannot give. So don't be troubled or afraid.*

So do not LET your heart be troubled, receive the gift of peace dear one. *For he himself is our peace,…* Ephesians 2:14 (NIV)

You, dear children, are from God and have overcome them, because the one who is in you is greater than the one who is in the world. 1 John 4:4 (NIV)

Please record one way God has impacted your heart with His Truth today.

_____

_____

_____

_____

Let go of your troubles to take hold of His peace. He has the victory and in Him, you do too.

Day 2: The Aftertaste of Hope

Hello, I'm glad you are here. The last verse we read yesterday in John 14 makes a great transition into our next chapter of study today. John 14:31 (NLT) *but I will do what the Father requires of me, so that the world will know that I love the Father. Come let's be going.* Please pray and come, let's keep studying.

Please read John chapter 15. ____

Come let's be going, we have a mission according to John 14:31 (above) to do what the Father requires of us SO THAT the world will know what?

_____

That we love God!

What is our mission? See John 15:4-5 for our answer.

_____

_____

Our mission is to put our relationship with God first, to abide in Him, walk with Him, remain in Him, in His Word and through constant prayer. Then He Himself will take care of the rest of the details of His mission for our lives.

It seems in John 15:2 there are two different things that the gardener can do to a branch on the vine. What are they?

_____

Cut off and prune. Why would a branch be cut off according to this verse?

_____

What would an unfruitful branch or life look like?

_____

Someone who chooses to reject God and causes others to be hindered from growing in Him. A bad branch can begin to infect the growth of others so a gardener cuts them out. HOWEVER there is also Romans 11:23!

Romans 11:23 (NIV) *And if they do not persist in unbelief, they will be grafted in, for God is able to graft them in again.*

God is able! Do you know someone maybe that seems to have cut themselves off from God? Keep praying for them dear one. God is able to graft them in again if they should turn and choose Him.

The other thing a gardener could do is prune. Pruning is when branches are cut back to promote more growth. God disciplines those He loves to strengthen us and refine our character. Pruning is not comfortable yet will produce more fruit in time if we patiently endure and receive His teaching. We are all in a growth process in Christ. All of us.

In John 15:11 Jesus tells us why He has told us these things. Please record why below.

_____

That we might have overflowing joy!! Joy because we have a lavish love so deep, long, high and wide we can not even begin to fathom it (Eph. 3:14-19). However it is our choice to remain in it or not. His love never goes away, His love is unfailing. He proved this by dying while we were still sinners unable to do anything to earn His eternal blessing. We, however, can choose to stop the overflowing joy of it to our hearts by rejecting His Way.

Jesus' command is clear in John 15:17. Please record it below.

_____

This command is impossible to do all the time with everyone, apart from Him. There are those that do not have His love truly in them and we will be confronted with hate.

John 15:18 urges us to remember what?

_____

We will not experience any hate that God didn't first experience and has the strength and wisdom for us to overcome IN Him.

Compare the fulfillment of Scripture in John 15:25 to Ps. 35:19, 69:4.

What does Psalm 64:9 say?

_____

The world will take notice of the contrast within us when we remain in Him and love even our enemies with His love.

What does John 15:26 assure us of?

_____

We will have the Holy Spirit to tend both our head and heart. Strengthening us in His power as well as teaching and guiding us. I pray that the Holy Spirit would stir within me as I read His Word so that the words are not just ink on a page but the life giving breath of God come to life in me. *But it is the spirit in a person, the breath of the Almighty, that gives them understanding.* Job 32:8 (NIV)

As we pray for more of His Spirit let's embark over to John chapter 16, our final Scripture for today. _____

Again verse 1 in John chapter 16 makes a wonderful transition from our last chapter. Why has Jesus told us all these things according to John 16:1?

_____

So we do not abandon the faith. When our ship starts to rock on the waves of doubt in the storm of the unknown, don't jump ship, rather cling to your Anchor! (Hebrews 6:19)

Why else is Jesus telling us these things according to John 16:4?

_____

So that we can go back to what we know, go back to what we REMEMBER is the Truth He has already spoken and apply it to our current situations!

Sometimes we can become troubled over seeking our A or B answer to prayer and we completely forget He has already given us the wisdom (James 1:5) to discern the right answer if we would just be still in Him (Ps. 46:10) and apply it!!

God has given us His Word and His Spirit even to help us remember. We don't have to rely on our own faulty minds to do that! Praise God! How many times have you walked into the next room only to forget why you're even there?!! But we do need to be faithful with inputting His Word so that when it comes time to recall something the Spirit has something to pull from in our vault of a mind.

Praise God we can go back to His Anchor in any storm! *We have this hope as an anchor for the soul, firm and secure....* Hebrews 6:19 (NIV) *...in quietness and trust is your strength, ...* Isaiah 30:15 (NIV)

I don't know about you but I find it comforting that even the disciples who talked with Jesus face to face still found themselves wondering in the middle of John 16:18 what I so often find myself exclaiming! Record what they were thinking in verse 18.

_____

Oh, we still just do not understand!

Yet in His infinite grace He responds to them in John 16:19 and beyond with compassion. He didn't even wait for them to voice their confusion! He could read their thoughts and just began meeting them where they were at with Truth! Verse 20 (NLT), *I tell you the truth,...*

What Truth did Jesus reveal in John 16:20?

_____

It was not an easy Truth to swallow but it had the aftertaste of Living Hope!!

All our situations and circumstances in Jesus have the aftertaste of Living Hope dear one.

The hope of a joy that cannot be taken from us! (Verse 22)

What do the disciples resolve to know at the end of this chapter? See John 16:30.

_____

(NLT) *Now we understand that you know everything, and there is no need to question you...*

Oh dear one, if we understand nothing else let's understand that He does!!!!

John 16:33 (NLT) I have told you all this SO THAT you may have peace IN me. Here on earth you WILL have many trials and sorrows. BUT TAKE heart, because I HAVE OVERCOME the world." (emphasis mine.)

Dear one, take heart, take peace, take the whole gift of Him in, by way of trusting Him who is higher than ourselves and our circumstance.

Please record what you want to remember most from today.

_____

_____

_____

_____

Day 3: Mission Possible

Welcome back to study today my friend. Today we will be walking through John chapter 17 which records what is known as Jesus' final prayer. Before we dig into His prayer let's say our prayers.

May He energize our commitment to study His Word and bring fresh perspective by His Spirit within us that we might understand great and unsearchable things we do not yet know, confirming His mission and His purpose for each of us that we might respond in faithful obedience.

Please meet me on the other side of John 17. _____

Wow! We live here in a battle zone of good against evil and it is true, prayer is a war room in which battles are waged and won!

John 17:4 indicates how glory was brought to the Father. Record how below.

_____

Might we be energized to do the same: complete the work He gives us to do! Again what good are our efforts apart from Him?! If we remain in Him, who completes the work started in our life? See Philippians 1:6.

_____

We won't miss our mission if we are enveloped in relationship with God, the Author of our mission.

In John 17:7 the disciples recognized something, what was it?

_____

Everything was a gift from above! Have we come to such a realization? Do our lives reflect that we believe it?

In verse 8 a progression is indicated. First the disciples were told the message of Truth, then they accepted the message of Jesus (Truth). Then they knew it. Then they believed it. TOLD, ACCEPT, KNOW, BELIEVE.

Romans 10:21 tells us He has held out His hand to a disobedient and obstinate people. Let us not be disobedient and obstinate but rather one who receives His amazing gift of grace to accept His message, to know it and to move into a sincere belief of it!

John 17:11 indicates there is power in His name. Can you think of a title that comes with power in your own world?

_____

There is no authority or power above God Almighty. John 13:3 tells us all authority had been given to Jesus. How do we respect His Authority by way of respecting the authorities He has allowed to remain in position (Dan. 2:21)? (This is not including the realm of authority that goes against God's way such as in abuse situations.)

_____

We don't have to like or agree with all those who are in authority but we are called to respect the authority God has allowed.

List ways Titus 3 gives us to live rightly under authority that has been placed over us and/or within a position of authority we ourselves are in.

_____

_____

_____

At the end of the day we answer to one Authority, the Author of all authority, and we want to be commended for our conduct having reflected Him well in all things.

Again in John 17:14 Jesus points back to remembering His Word. Just as Jesus tells us in this world we will have trouble He knew about the one to betray Him through the Scriptures. See Psalm 41:9

John 17:13-15 indicates Jesus gave us something, had intention to fill us with something and also asks the Father for something. What are those three somethings?

_____

_____

He gave us His Word, that we might be filled with His joy and He asks not that we are taken out of the world but that we would be protected as world changers within it!

John 17 is not only a prayer for His disciples but what do verses 20-24 indicate Jesus prays for those who would believe in Him through their message (a.k.a. US!!)?

_____

_____

_____

The fact that God is praying for us, has prayed for us, should give us confidence as we carry out our God given mission here on earth to make His name and glory renown through our praise!

John 17:26 ends Jesus' prayer with His final thought. What is it?

_____

His desire is that the love the Father has for Him would indwell us! This love and phenomenon surpasses anything the world would have to offer us! As we abide in His love the world will see contrast and He will be magnified for all the world to see and know that what they crave to fill the void in their heart is found in Jesus alone.

From one man he made all the nations, that they should inhabit the whole earth; and he marked out their appointed times in history and the boundaries of their lands. God did this so that they would seek him and perhaps reach out for him and find him, though he is not far from any one of us. Acts 17:26-27 (NIV)

You have been designed and equipped for a mighty purposeful mission! Today let's set our hearts and minds on things above and re-commit, that He might re-confirm His loving presence (by His amazing grace) within us making all missions possible.

In the same way, the Spirit helps us in our weakness. We do not know what we ought to pray for, but the Spirit himself intercedes for us through wordless groans. Romans 8:26 (NIV) *Who then is the one who condemns? No one. Christ Jesus who died—more than that, who was raised to life—is at the right hand of God and is also interceding for us.* Romans 8:34 (NIV)

Please record what you would like to remember most from today's study.

_____

_____

_____

_____

Day 4: Rise, Surrendered As A Living Sacrifice

Welcome dear one. Thank you for your commitment to studying His Word with such diligence, I know that is an answer to prayer! I'm sure along the way you have had to make sacrifices to dedicate so much time to such an in-depth study. Remember 1 Samuel 2:30 (NIV) in which God says, ...*Those who honor me I will honor,*...

Today we will walk through a garden. A garden of agony from which will spring up for us an eternal garden of paradise. May our study of Him today produce in us a pleasing aroma of His Son as we ask that He conform us more into His image and that He strengthen our trust and faith that we might not fall away on account of how He chooses to bring about His glory through our lives.

For as the earth brings forth its sprouts, and as a garden causes what is sown in it to sprout up, so the Lord GOD will cause righteousness and praise to sprout up before all the nations. Isaiah 61:11 (ESV)

Please pray and then meet me on the other side of Matthew 26:36-46 _____, Mark 14:32-42 _____, and Luke 22:39-46. _____

Mark 14:32 (NLT) indicates they went to the olive grove called Gethsemane. Gethsemane in Aramaic means oil press and here Jesus would be pressed and poured out in anguish and agony for our sake.

What did Jesus ask the disciples to do while He prayed in Mark 14:32?

_____

Sit. Is there anything in our lives we need to let sit in order to spend time at our heavenly Father's feet?

_____

_____

Things gleaned through time spent with God are things that can never be taken from us.

Jesus took three disciples with Him. Who were they according to Matthew 26:37?

_____

What insight can you glean from Hebrews 10:24-25 and Ecclesiastes 4:10 regarding companionship or fellowship with other believers?

_____

Matthew 26:37-38 gives insight into how Jesus was feeling at this moment. Describe His emotional state as you see it portrayed in these verses.

_____

Oh dear one, He knows pain and suffering to the greatest degree, He has experienced a soul …*crushed with grief to the point of death….* Matt. 26:38 (NLT)

What does Hebrews 5:7-9 remind us of that can bring comfort to us in our time of anguish?

_____

He made a way through His own crushing to be our sure Light at the end of every dark tunnel.

In the olive grove He experienced a hard pressing and as an olive must be pressed to bring out the oil for lamps, Jesus, through His surrender and sacrifice became our Light, resurrection and life.

Psalm 42:5-6 gives us advice for when our soul is downcast. Where do we put our hope and what shall we remember?

_____

How many times did Jesus pray for a different way for the cost of our sin to be paid?

_____

Three times. Please read 2 Corinthians 12:7-9 and record the number of times Paul prayed for the removal of his "thorn" and the answer he received from God.

_____

Jesus submitted to the Father's authority though it cost Him greatly, He trusted His Father's grace to be faithfully sufficient to sustain Him. Remember

Hebrews 12:2. How and what did Jesus set His focus on to get Him through?

Remember in John 14:1-4 we found Jesus giving us the secret of patient endurance… Trust. Trust His promises as we walk through the process WITH His promised presence. Jesus had to go through a separation of His Father to carry our sin to the grave in our place. We who accept and believe in Him will never have to face a trial alone, never have to experience the depth of anguish He did because, He did. He carried our worst of the worst, our cross, all the way to hell for us, in our place.

Jesus went that deep for us. Now we never ever have to carry the pressing weight of this world alone. The pressure we are under will never superseded His power to stand up under it. He will be our sufficiency in all things because His will in the garden was surrendered in order to become a living sacrifice for us. His "no" was for our greater "yes". Paul's "no" was for a greater "yes" and God's grace was sufficient.

Who might receive a greater "yes" through our "no" (a "no" we have not been asked to carry alone) in our own garden of suffering? Will we surrender to the One who surrendered for us? His surrender won a room for us in His eternal Kingdom too great for human description! 1 Corinthians 2:9 (NIV) *However, as it is written: "What no eye has seen, what no ear has heard, and what no human mind has conceived"— the things God has prepared for those who love him—*

We are hard pressed on every side, but not crushed; perplexed, but not in despair; persecuted, but not abandoned; struck down, but not destroyed. 2 Corinthians 4:8-9 (NIV)

What did those disciples do that were asked to sit with Him? See Luke 22:45.

The fell asleep. In this crucial hour Jesus finds those He is going to sacrifice Himself for, sleeping! Yet even then Jesus encourages them with teaching! He saw from His position of grief the details of others suffering! He knew they would be up against the greatest temptation to feel like it had all been a cruel joke watching Him die soon. He saw through His own anguish to encourage His men in theirs.

What does He encourage them to do so as not to fall into temptation?

_____

Pray! Pray, summon the powers of Heaven to defend you against the schemes of the enemy! When we don't understand, exhausted from anguish and grief prayer is our weapon and when we have no words the Spirit within us will intercede. (See Romans 8:26-27.)

Luke 22:42 Records Jesus submitting to the Father's will which is anything but a passive move. Often it takes more strength to submit than to assert your own will.

Luke 22:43 tells us who came and ministered to Him?

_____

Angels. Jesus humbly received ministering from angels who were clearly below Him in rank! Who might God want to minister to you through that you never would have expected? He can use anyone to encourage us, let us not discount those He would bring across our path to encourage and teach us just because they aren't what we expected. He could use that irritatingly negative person, He could use that child… We can learn from anyone so let's be open to His will, His way.

In Matthew 26:46 Jesus gives a direction, what is it?

_____

If it were me, I might have said, Up let's run!! But there at the "oil press" Jesus prayed and received strength to say, *Rise! Let us go! Here comes my betrayer!"* (NIV), to rise and face the trial in sufficient grace.

Dear one, Jesus submitted to the Father and rose to faced the greatest trial so that we too in His presence could rise through anything in this life. Submitting our will to trust His higher way affords sustaining strength and all sufficient grace. *But he was pierced for our transgressions, he was crushed for our iniquities; the punishment that brought us peace was on him, and by his wounds we are healed.* Isaiah 53:5 (NIV)

Pleases record what impacted your heart the most from your study today.

_____

_____

_____

_____

Day 5: Faith Steps Forward, God-Confident

Welcome friend. Thank you for your diligence in pursuing God's heart. He rewards those who earnestly seek Him (Hebrews 11:6). Let's praise Him for that as we begin in prayer.

Please continue through this next segment of Scriptures. Matthew 26:47-56 _____, Mark 14:43-52 _____, Luke 22:47-53 _____, and John 18:1-11. _____

John 18:4 in the NLT states, *Jesus fully realized all that was going to happen to him, so he stepped forward...*

He knew and didn't run but stayed and not only stayed but stepped forward in the hard thing for you and for me!!

As He set the example for us first, His Word tells us in Hebrews 10:35, 39 that in Christ we are not of those who shrink back! It tells us not to throw away our confidence for we will be richly rewarded! Dear one, how much God-confidence have you stepped forward in? All we need is all available to us in Him! Share a time if you will, of when you did step forward in God-confidence and experienced His all sufficient grace.

_____

_____

May this memory of His faithfulness to you embolden your faith and trust in Him for your next forward step in God-confidence.

Flipping back to Matthew's gospel for a moment, what does Jesus call His betrayer in 26:50?

_____

Friend! He calls Judas, friend. Jesus loved Judas in spite of His sin. God hates the sin but loves the sinner if only we could take hold of that hope! It's the hope of redemption He sacrificed Himself to gift us! All of us.

While we are in Matthew chapter 26 both verse 54 and 56 point us back to the fulfillment of what?

_____

The fulfillment of Scripture! Jesus was always doing that, fulfilling Scripture!

Take a glance at some of the following Scriptures as further proof that Jesus always had the upper hand. He was in total control the entire time, fulfilling that which was foretold long before He came to earth. Jesus gave His life for ours, nothing was taken from Him that He did not first consent to give. Jesus was here on assignment and was faithful every hard step of the way.

Psalm 22:7-8, 16-18 __

Isaiah 53:7-9 __

Zechariah 13:7 __

1 Peter 1:10-11 __ This Scripture from the New Testament speaking of the Old Testament predictions fulfilled in Jesus our Messiah.

In John 18:5 who does Jesus say He is?

_____

I AM! He uses the name for Himself given in Exodus 3:14! And with this proclamation what happened? (See verse 6.)

_____

They fell down. One way or another every knee will bow! May we choose to do so willingly before we must be forced. *That at the name of Jesus every knee should bow, in heaven and on earth and under the earth, and every tongue acknowledge that Jesus Christ is Lord, to the glory of God the Father.* Philippians 2:10-11 (NIV)

In John 18:10 what does Peter do to the high priest's servant, Malchus?

_____

Malchus means king - what a contrast held up here between worldly kingdom values and that of our True King of all kings! Luke, the physician records how Jesus reaches out and touches His enemy and heals him!! (Luke 22:51) Again we see Jesus walking the talk; B*ut among you it will be different...* Luke 22:26 (NLT)

Jesus was a different King than the world was used to or even expected. He came to heal and seek and save the lost through humble submission to the Father's will in becoming a living sacrifice.

How can we magnify our King and His Kingdom? By living as He did in humble submission to our King of kings. Becoming a living sacrifice day by day, moment by moment in His all sufficient grace until we reach our glorious heavenly home. It will all be worth it dear one, every last hard step will be worth it.

...And surely I am with you always, to the very end of the age." Matthew 28:20 (NIV)

Please record what you would like to remember most from today.

_____

_____

_____

_____

Day 6 & 7: A Time To Reflect

Over the next two days take time to reflect over your week of study. Maybe you need some time to catch up on the study material and this might be the perfect break to do just that with the Lord!

I encourage you to glance back at the final point at the end of each day that you recorded having had the greatest impact on your heart. As you spend time with God in prayer, reflect and record on the lines below how God is tying it all together and applying it to your life.

Ask that God make it clear who He would have you invite into a natural opportunity to share Him, to apply what you are learning. Trust Him to continue to take the lead. May we have a heart ever ready with eyes and ears out to the opportunities God wants to invite us into for His glory and praise.

Do not merely listen to the word, and so deceive yourselves. Do what it says. Anyone who listens to the word but does not do what it says is like someone who looks at his face in a mirror and, after looking at himself, goes away and immediately forgets what he looks like. But whoever looks intently into the perfect law that gives freedom, and continues in it - not forgetting what they have heard, but doing it - they will be blessed in what they do. James 1:22-25 (NIV)

_____

_____

_____

_____

_____

Philippians 4:13 (NIV) *I can do all things through him who gives me strength.*

John 14:26 (NIV) *But the Advocate, the Holy Spirit, whom the Father will send in my name, will teach you all things and will remind you of everything I have said to you.*

WEEK 6

I am coming soon. Hold on to what you have, so that no one will take your crown. The one who is victorious I will make a pillar in the temple of my God. Never again will they leave it. I will write on them the name of my God and the name of the city of my God, the new Jerusalem, which is coming down out of heaven from my God; and I will also write on them my new name. Revelation 3:11-12 (NIV)

Day 1: Flashback To Comeback

Hello friend! Now that we have made it halfway through our 10 week study together, lets think back over our time for just a quick moment (flashback). Off the top of your head what point does your brain flashback to as your favorite thing we have studied so far?

Flashback memory:

_____

_____

I hope that brief flashback has encouraged you to embark boldly into today's study and finish strong this week in order to add to your treasure bank of Truth! Let's bow in prayer, submitting to God Almighty's leadership before beginning.

Please meet me now on the other side of some Scripture. This is the bulk of our reading today so just sit back and savor the four different angles with which this scene is portrayed. There is just no book more thrilling than His living Word!

John 18:12-27 _____ Luke 22:54-65 _____ Mark 14:53-72 _____ and Matthew 26:57-75 _____

Do you feel the intensity building too?!!

Beginning in Mark's gospel account where did they take Jesus after He was arrested in the garden?

_____

The high priest's home.

John's gospel tells us He was taken to Annas, the father in law of Caiaphas who at that time was the high priest. This was the very same Caiaphas whom God used to prophesy that one man would die for all back in John 11:49-51!

God is always moving (John 5:17) and nothing and no one will be able to thwart His plan (Job 42:2). Do you believe this? Do you believe no mean person, lie, rumor or failure can stump or trump God's plan for you?

God, the Author of time, doesn't waste a moment. His Kingdom plan (which includes you and I) is rolling out even as we sit here!

According to Mark 14:54 where was Peter warming himself?

John's gospel depicts the exact type of fire which will be important in the future to know... see John 18:18 and record the type of fire Peter was warming himself by.

A charcoal fire.

In Mark 14:55 was the group at Annas house looking for Truth? YES   NO

What does Jeremiah 29:13 tell us again?

Those that are truly seeking Truth will find Him. However sometimes like these religious leaders, Truth is not truly what people are seeking. Sometimes they are only looking for excuses not to believe. Excuses in any situation are lurking around every corner and under every rock so you will find what you look for, be it an excuse or Truth you will find it.

As we proceed in Mark 14 verses 56-59 many false witnesses came forward but no one could get their stories straight! How did Jesus respond to all the false accusations (verse 61)?

He was silent. How was Jesus fulfilling Scripture even in His silence? See Isaiah 53:7 and 1 Peter 2:23.

How can we follow Scripture when we are falsely accused? Here are a few Scriptures to help you with your answer if you would like. Romans 12:19, James 1:2-4, Proverbs 11:9, Isaiah 54:17, 1 Peter 3:9, Proverbs 19:9, Luke 6:27, 1 Thessalonians 5:15, Proverbs 30:5

_____

_____

There is plenty of advice in the Bible on this as God knew human nature (John 2:24) and how hard it is to endure false accusations.

1 Corinthians 15:33 (NIV) *Do not be misled: "Bad company corrupts good character."* You can't always choose your company, but a lot of the time you can and when you can't, you can choose to exercise God's wisdom of which He pours out generously without finding fault. (James 1:5)

"I am sending you out like sheep among wolves. Therefore be as shrewd as snakes and as innocent as doves. Matthew 10:16 (NIV)

When Jesus is asked in Mark 14:61 just who He is, what is His response in verse 62?

_____

Friends, the great I AM is coming back for us just as He said!! For further confirmation check out Daniel 7:13, Acts 1:11, 1 Thessalonians 4:16, 2 Thessalonians 1:7, and Revelation 1:7, Revelation 22:20.

Meanwhile… let's glance out the window into the courtyard.

Let's look at this scene from Luke's perspective in Luke 22:54-62.

In verse 54 from where was Peter following?

_____

A distance. What might cause distance to occur between God and us?

_____

Sin, selfishness… How might we make an effort to close the distance if we notice one growing?

_____

Draw near to God, and he will draw near to you. Cleanse your hands, you sinners, and purify you hearts, you double-minded. James 4:8 (ESV)

We see that Jesus' prediction of Peter's denial of Him before the rooster crowed (Luke 22:34) comes true, because all God's Words are True (Prov. 30:5).

To refresh our memory please re-read Luke 22:31-34. _____

At the very moment the rooster crowed in Luke 22:60 what flashed back in Peter's mind?! See verse 61.

_____

The way Luke records this touches my heart deeply. Luke 22:61 (NLT) *At that moment the Lord turned and looked at Peter….*

When the Lord saw her, his heart overflowed with compassion. "Don't cry!" he said. Luke 7:13 (NLT)

Remembering back to just how Jesus presented to Peter the events of his failure in Luke 22 before they even happened… and how it was with hope that Peter would return to Him and fulfill the purpose that had not been thwarted by his downfall. This memory leads me to believe that it was with the same eyes, overflowing with compassion, that God saw the woman in Luke 7, that He now gazed upon Peter with in that very moment.

Deeply compassionate eyes engulfing Peter… both hearts breaking under the pain. Yet Jesus looks at him with eyes that speak, "Don't cry dear one, return to Me and strengthen your brothers! I'm dying to set you free from guilt and shame! Return to Me!!"

Luke 22:62 tells us Peter left the courtyard, weeping bitterly.

There is a difference between worldly sorrow in which we will soon see Judas experience and that of godly sorrow that we see Peter partake in.

2 Corinthians 7:10 (NIV) *Godly sorrow brings repentance that leads to salvation and leaves no regret, but worldly sorrow brings death.*

If you feel comfortable please share if you have experienced a time of godly sorrow in your life that brought about repentance and refinement.

I hope this memory encourages you. Just as Peter's mind in his moment of weakness flashed back to Jesus' words, he would have had to have remembered not only Jesus' prediction of failure... but also that they had been tied to His prediction of hope! Don't forget too, that it was Peter, Jesus had a conversation with about forgiveness being infinite back in Matthew 18:21-22.

Dear one no failure is too big, no pit is too deep that God can not redeem, reach and restore! *The LORD answered Moses, "Is the LORD's arm too short? …* Numbers 11:23 (NIV)

In closing today please savor all of Psalm 103. I pray you know the Truth that all your negative flashbacks are coupled with redeeming hope in Jesus dear one. It's His free gift to you held out with both nail scarred hands and compassion flooding His eyes. Return to Me and strengthen your brothers and sisters.

Jesus died and rose again to set us free! And who the Son sets free is free indeed! (John 8:36) Do you need to return? Oh dear one, you know the Way!

Psalm 103:4 NIV *who redeems your life from the pit and crowns you with love and compassion,*

Please record the point you want to remember most from today.

_____

_____

_____

_____

Thank you for today. God bless you muchly~

Day 2: When You've Tried All In The Trial

I will give him the honors of a victorious soldier, because he exposed himself to death. He was counted among the rebels. He bore the sins of many and interceded for rebels. Isaiah 53:12 (NLT)

Hello my friend. Today we enter into the trials, the unfair trials Jesus endured. If any of us feel we have been or are under pressure we can know for certain we have a Savior that understands just how we feel. He knows the strength we will need to endure and is ready with His all sufficient grace to be our Source of all we need. Let's praise Him for being a God who knows how to supply for our need before we know we even have a need! When the trial has tried our all He is our well of enduring perseverance that runs deeper still. There is no wound that goes deeper than His healing, no sin that goes beyond his redemption or need that goes beyond His provision. May God Almighty the great I Am lead us deeper still into more of Him with the grace to follow faithfully.

We will take this a step at a time. Please pray and meet me on the other side of Matthew 27:1-2 _____, Mark 15:1 _____ and Luke 22:66-71. _____

What time of day is this trial beginning?

_____

Early in the morning. The enemy doesn't sleep but neither does our God. He is always working so, in peace we can lie down and sleep, for our God alone makes us dwell in safety. (Psalm 4:8)

Each new day is a gift. Each day we can wake grateful that our God has not slept but that He kept us in safety while the spiritual battles rage on. He has given us night, a moment of rest, an opportunity to receive His peace and to recharge for the next day. So when our feet hit the ground in the morning the enemy says to himself, "Oh no, they're up!", as we ask God to show us our assignments this day.

Psalm 90:14 (NIV) *Satisfy us in the morning with your unfailing love, that we may sing for joy and be glad all our days.*

These leaders were all gathering to do what?

_____

Make their plans to accuse Jesus. Proverbs 16:9 (NIV) tell us, *In their hearts humans plan their course, but the Lord establishes their steps.*

According to Mark 15:1 who were they taking Jesus to?

_____

How convenient that Pilate was in town! Why did the Jews need to send Jesus to the Roman governor? Well, the Romans would not allow the Jews to incite capital punishment so they needed Jesus to be sentenced by a Roman leader. This posed a problem in that Rome would not find their accusations of Jesus enough to crucify Him so they had to conjure up additional accusations that would get the Romans attention. Claiming to be king, posing a threat to Caesar would get Roman attention.

In Luke 22:69 Jesus refers to Psalm 110. Take a moment to read that Psalm. If that first verse was running through His head at that time I wonder if any other part of that Psalm was giving Him encouragement? What parts stand out to you as most encouraging?

_____

_____

You will rule over your enemies (vs. 2) your strength renewed day by day (vs. 3) The Lord stands at your right hand to protect you (vs. 5) He will be victorious (vs. 7) are just a few stanzas (NLT) I glean encouragement from!

What Truth's and promises run through your mind when you are facing difficulty? Do you have any verses or stories committed to memory from the Bible that offer specific encouragement to you in times of distress or trial?

_____

_____

I can do all things through Christ who strengthens me. Philippians 4:13 (NKJV)

Luke 22:70 was all the evidence the religious leaders needed. They could accuse Him of blaspheme (claiming to be God) but in this case it truly was not blaspheme for Jesus was telling the Truth. He even used the I Am statement the leaders would have recognized as God's name for Himself given in Ex. 3:14. ... *"You say that I am."* Luke 22:70 (NLT)

Please read a bit further in Matthew chapter 27. Verses 3-10. _____

Verse 3 tells us Judas was filled with what?

_____

Remorse not necessarily repentance. Only God knows the depths of Judas' heart. However true repentance results in a change of heart and restoration in relationship with God.

In verse 4 Judas does what?

_____

He confesses his sin to the priest. The priest's job was to help those caught in sin, to guide, teach and lead them to God but here we see no such thing occur. Humans are humans and fallible and faulty. May we never let our view of God be distorted by imperfect humans. We have a perfect God and nothing and no one will ever be able to change that.

What encouragement do you receive from the following verses?
Isaiah 9:6 and Hebrews 4:14-16

_____

_____

We have The Wonderful Counselor, a great high priest who can sympathize with us and we can approach with confidence to receive mercy and find grace!!

I will instruct you and teach you in the way you should go; I will counsel you with my loving eye on you. Psalm 32:8 (NIV)

What does Judas do in Matthew 27:5?

_____

This the result of a guilt stricken conscience - what a tragedy!!! The Old Testament law Deut. 19:16-21, was fulfilled by Judas' death. He apparently took his own punishment into his own hands rather than run to Jesus. Jesus died to cleanse us of our guilty conscience and to set us free from the law of sin and death.

Romans 8:2 (NIV) *because through Christ Jesus the law of the Spirit who gives life has set you free from the law of sin and death.*

Hebrews 10:22 (NIV) *let us draw near to God with a sincere heart and with the full assurance that faith brings, having our hearts sprinkled to cleanse us from a guilty conscience and having our body washed with pure water.*

Let's not discount the immensity of Christ's sacrifice for us. There is nothing His blood will not cover if we humbly offer it over to Him. *As far as the east is from the west, so far has he removed our transgression from us.* Psalm 103:12 (NIV) Do not let the enemy of your soul outwit you! *If we confess our sins, he is faithful and just and will forgive us our sins and purify us from all unrighteousness.* 1 John 1:9 (NIV) Live in the Truth of His Victory for you!!!

Please record what made the greatest impact on your heart today as you studied His Word of Truth.

_____

_____

_____

_____

Day 3: His Whisper

Hello friend. Today I sit at my desk listening to the whispering winds whip through the tree branches that are just beginning to bud with new life! This reminds me of God's ever present power. Though I cannot see the wind I see the effects of it's strength and with that God whispers to my heart, I Am here.

Let's praise Him for His faithful presence as we bow before His leadership today beginning in prayer.

After praying please begin in the following passages: Matthew 27:11-14 _____, Mark 15:2-5 _____, Luke 23:1-12 _____ and John 18:28-37. _____

In Matthew 27:12-13 what was Pilate surprised at?

_____

That Jesus would remain silent before such accusations. Yet what does Isaiah 53:7 show us Jesus exemplified?

_____

Again, He was committed to completing the mission for which the Father had sent Him and was depicted in the Truth of Scripture. He was a beautiful picture of self-assurance and peace that comes from trusting in God.

How has Scripture emboldened you to know the Way when you can't understand or see all the steps in your journey?

_____

_____

Matthew 27:13 in the NLT starts, *"Don't you hear…"* Don't you hear all the negative things and accusations swirling around you? We can ask ourselves the same question and our answer can be according to how closely we walk and trust God. What do you hear? There will always be two voices in your head so to speak, one a lie and one Truth. May His Truth be our loudest reality and the voice we lean into. Often He whispers, not so that it's hard to hear Him but so that we might press into Him. Thus increasing the intimacy of our relationship with Him.

The "thorns" of hurtful people, words or circumstances can pierce us or pin us. They pierced Jesus so that we can choose to allow our "thorns" to pin us closer to His heart and voice of Truth. Just because our situation seems to have stopped our music doesn't mean we have to stop dancing right!

Genesis 50:20 (NIV) *You intended to harm me, but God intended it for good to accomplish what is now being done, the saving of many lives.*

How have you heard His whispers to you?

_____

_____

Luke 23:7 records that Pilate, trying to escape a sticky situation, sends Jesus to Herod who was in town for Passover, the same Herod who had John the Baptist killed. This pleased Herod as he had been curious about Jesus just as he had been about John.

Both men declare Jesus innocent fulfilling Isaiah 53:11. Jesus was the innocent suffering servant.

Pilate was not the most popular guy so he did not want to risk his political position by allowing a riot to occur in his province. He saw Jesus more of a political threat than anything else.

When stakes are high it can be difficult to discern right from wrong. We may slip into worldly wisdom rather than using God's wisdom. How do we know we are using God's wisdom? See James 3:17.

_____

_____

This verse offers us a good checklist to pull out when our judgment might be skewed in certain situations.

Please look at four different segments of Scripture and record the different ways Pilate attempts to deal with Jesus.

John 18:31
_____
Pass Him off.

John 18:39
_____
Find an excuse.

John 19:1-6
_____
Compromise with a flogging.

John 19:15-16
_____
Appeal to human sympathy.

None of us can let others decide what to do about Jesus for us, every breathing soul must decide for themself to accept Jesus as their Savior God. (No decision is a decision.) Jesus tells us plainly… John 14:6 (NIV) *Jesus answered, "I am the way and the truth and the life. No one comes to the Father except through me.* John 3:16 (NIV) *For God so loved the world that he gave his one and only Son, that whoever believes in him shall not perish but have eternal life.*

How do you respond under pressure? 2 Corinthians 4:7-10 (NIV) holds out a Truth we can anchor our souls to. *But we have this treasure in jars of clay to show that this all-surpassing power is from God and not from us. We are hard pressed on every side, but not crushed; perplexed, but not in despair; persecuted, but not abandoned; struck down, but not destroyed. We always carry around in our body the death of Jesus, so that the life of Jesus may also be revealed in our body.*

The One who stood for you, stands with you.
He whispers, "You are not ever alone."

Have I not commanded you? Be strong and courageous. Do not be afraid; do not be discouraged, for the Lord your God will be with you wherever you go." Joshua 1:9 (NIV)

Please record the most impactful point to your heart today.

_____

_____

_____

_____

Day 4: When Under Pressure

Hello my friend! I'm very glad you have persevered through all the pressures that may have pulled and tugged you away from your quiet time with God today. I commend you for making it here! I pray you feel His blessings over your faithful pursuit of His heart that faithfully is in pursuit of yours. Let's begin in prayer thanking Him for when the pressures rise around us we can always press deeper into Him. May He press us onward into His Truth today.

Let's wrap ourselves up cozy in the warmth of His Word beginning with Matthew 27:15-26 _____, Mark 15:6-15 _____, Luke 23:13-25 _____ and John 18:38-19:16. _____

Ironically Barabbas was guilty of the crime Jesus was being falsely accused of. Barabbas was set free while Jesus was crucified. Such a picture of what the cross accomplished for us. Jesus, yet innocent, bore our sins and took our cross so we could go free.

In John 19:11 Who ultimately had the power in this situation?

_____

God. God had temporarily allowed Pilate control so that Jesus could advance to the cross. What might God be using in your life to ultimately advance His purpose in your life?

_____

God is never off His throne, out of ideas, or scrambling for plan B. He's got you dear one in the palm of His mighty, unshakable, nail scarred, victorious hand.

My Father, who has given them to me, is greater than all; no one can snatch them out of my Father's hand. John 10:29 (NIV)

Pilate took what seat in John 19:13?

_____

The judgment seat. When questioned or ridiculed because of your faith know that although you may be on trial before your accusers, they will ultimately be on trial before The Judge. Remember Matthew 5:11-12!

As Jesus called Judas "friend" at the moment he kissed Him to betray Him, God also offers a way out for Pilate. He truly is the Father of all compassion, comfort and mercies (2 Cor. 1:3)! In Matthew 27:19 while Pilate is seated on his judgment seat before Jesus who is sent in to try and dissuade Pilate from condemning Jesus? And what did she have to say?

_____

_____

What does James 1:13 and 1 Corinthians 10:13 tell us?

_____

It doesn't say we won't be handed more than we can bare but rather we will not be tempted beyond what we can bare. When we are tempted He is faithful and will provide us a way out. It also does not say, that way out will be easy. But the same God who comes along side us to shoulder that which is too heavy for us to bare, is also the God who walks with us through every way out of temptation if we're willing to take it.

When we are handed more than we can handle He promises to be our all sufficient grace to bring us through (2 Cor. 12:9). We will not be crushed, He has shoulders big enough to carry what we can't but we must walk closely enough to Him so that we can share in His yoke.

Please read Matthew 11:28-30. _____

Of all the words God could have used to describe Himself, what two words does He choose in Matthew 11:29?

_____

Gentle and humble.

Dear one, we have a God who was crushed so that we would not have to be. When under pressure, come under the iron clad trustworthy umbrella of His Word and find rest for your soul.

Please record what you want to remember most from today's study.

_____
_____
_____
_____

Day 5: Times Of Refreshing

Welcome friend. As I sit here I'm gazing through our big front room windows at the gentle spring rain refreshes the air like nothing else ever could. There is just no match for the smell of God's rain is there?! Actually my youngest son just charged through the back porch doorway exclaiming, "IT SMELLS SO GOOD!!!"

Let's pause and thank God for the refreshment of His Word that rejuvenates a soul even in the driest seasons of life.

Please meet me on the other side of Matthew 27:27-31 _____ and Mark 15:16-19. _____

These passages indicate that it was the whole company of soldiers that was called together to mock Jesus. That doesn't sound like a small few.

What did they dress Him in?

_____

A purple robe.

What was put on His head?

_____

A crown of thorns.

What did they do and say to Him?

_____

_____

They were mocking His claim to be King. This was allowed to advance God's plan however what does Galatians 6:7 tell us?

_____

_____

Don't be deceived dear one… you too are on victory's side because of what Jesus endured on our behalf. How ever you have been mocked for your faith has not gone unnoticed. The God who experienced it first hand knows how you feel, and has all you need to endure, so that in the end you receive His very great reward.

Philippians 2:9-11 tells us what? How does this encourage you knowing you're on His team, functioning from that same victory won?

_____

Please read 1 Samuel 30:1-6. _____

What happens to these men, David included?

_____

How are they emotionally?

_____

What does David resolve to do (verse 6)?

_____

And David was greatly distressed, for the people spoke of stoning him, because all the people were bitter in soul, each for his sons and daughters. But David strengthened himself in the LORD his God. 1 Sam. 30:6 (ESV)

But David strengthened himself in the Lord his God. Strengthened himself. How might one strengthen himself in God?

_____

_____

Take a moment and read 2 Samuel 16:5-14. _____

Who is mocked in this story?

_____

King David.

How did he deal with this (verse 12)?

_____

He trusted God.

What happens in verse 14?

_____

And the king, and all people who were with him, arrived weary at the Jordan. And there he refreshed himself. 2 Sam. 16:14 (ESV)

I wonder if here David refreshed himself in a similar way as before. He came to the Jordan that had been parted for his people in the past. Please read Joshua 4:4-7. _____

I wonder if David's eye caught the stones piled up as a memorial to God's faithfulness in his past, refreshing his faith in his present.

What remembrance of God's faithfulness do you have that stands as a memorial emboldening your faith today?

_____

_____

It was at the water of the Jordan that David refreshed himself. We have the invitation to come and be refreshed in the free gift of the water of life!

Revelation 22:17 (NIV) *The Spirit and the bride say, "Come!" And let the one who hears say, "Come!" Let the one who is thirsty come; and let the one who wishes take the free gift of the water of life.*

Oh dear one, let's be refreshed by His free gift of the water of life, His Word, His faithful promises and fellowship with Him in prayer. *that times of refreshing may come from the presence of the Lord, and that he may send the Christ appointed for you, Jesus,* Acts 3:20 (ESV)

Please recored what has impacted your heart the most from your time today in His Word.

_____

_____

_____

_____

Day 6 & 7: A Time To Reflect

Over the next two days take time to reflect over your week of study. Maybe you need some time to catch up on the study material and this might be the perfect break to do just that with the Lord!

I encourage you to glance back at the final point at the end of each day that you recorded having had the greatest impact on your heart. As you spend time with God in prayer, reflect and record on the lines below how God is tying it all together and applying it to your life.

Ask that God make it clear who He would have you invite into a natural opportunity to share Him, to apply what you are learning. Trust Him to continue to take the lead. May we have a heart ever ready with eyes and ears out to the opportunities God wants to invite us into for His glory and praise.

Do not merely listen to the word, and so deceive yourselves. Do what it says. Anyone who listens to the word but does not do what it says is like someone who looks at his face in a mirror and, after looking at himself, goes away and immediately forgets what he looks like. But whoever looks intently into the perfect law that gives freedom, and continues in it - not forgetting what they have heard, but doing it - they will be blessed in what they do. James 1:22-25 (NIV)

_____

_____

_____

_____

Philippians 4:13 (NIV) _I can do all things through him who gives me strength._

John 14:26 (NIV) *But the Advocate, the Holy Spirit, whom the Father will send in my name, will teach you all things and will remind you of everything I have said to you.*

WEEK 7

To the one who is victorious, I will give the right to sit with me on my throne, just as I was victorious and sat down with my Father on his throne. Revelation 3:21 (NIV)

Day 1: The Cup

Welcome to week 7! Thank you for your diligence in continuing your study of His heart!

So… we've traveled some distance together wouldn't you say, you and I over the past few weeks in the Word… Not sure if we are at the point of sharing intimate details or rather personal horror stories yet so if you're not quite ready to hear this one, you might want to skip to the paragraph after next.

Anyone else out there ever dropped their urine sample cup… all over the office floor right before you place it on the counter… so now you neither have a urine sample or any more urine left in you to leave a new one?!!! That being the least of your worries as you desperately seek out some paper towels... to just wrap yourself up in and die!!
I'm just asking… you know… for a friend.

So there are just some "cup's" in life you really would rather let go of and one's maybe you should hold onto a bit tighter!!! Today we will be getting into the hypothetical cups spoken of in Scripture. I tell you what, nothing compares to life in Christ! Our cup runs over in blessings; God is our biggest adventure, our greatest thrill and deepest love! Before we begin let's pray, praising Him who faithfully leads us in this life, never leaving us even in our most humbling moments and offers us a free cup refill anytime.

It is true that in Christ our "cup" is not half full or half empty... it's refillable! Praise Him!!!

Please head with me now to Matthew 27:32-34 _____, Mark 15:20-23 _____, Luke 23:26-32 _____ and John 19:16-17. _____

Here in John we see a second beating. The first is recorded in John 19:1 which was probably Pilate's attempt to show that Jesus had been punished and could go free however that is not how events transpired. Jesus was whipped, mocked and presented before the people (John 19:5). When the people relentlessly cried crucify Him, Pilate, in John 19:16, has Jesus prepared for crucifixion which would have included a second beating bringing Him near death.

Luke 23:26-32 is the only gospel that records Jesus addressing the tears of the women. Even in His agony He noticed and took the time to address the emotional state of others. Knowing the hardship that would continue to come for all humanity and that what He was doing now would be the only way made for us to escape the brokenness of this world, may have emboldened His resolve to continue forward. Has any wrong in your life emboldened your resolve to make it right rather than to back down?

_____

In our agony and own distress may God give us the grace to look up, notice and follow through on addressing the needs of others. What are the effects of this kind of service? See Isaiah 58:10.

_____

Mark 15:21 tells us there was a certain individual who happened to just be passing by at the moment Jesus was in need of someone to carry His cross. What is this man's name, where was he from and what are his son's names?

Cyrene is in northern Africa. He may have saved up for a long time to be able to afford such a trip to Jerusalem and experience the Passover celebration in that city. Who could have imagined that of all people a guy from northern Africa would be the guy pulled forward to carry the cross of Christ?! Can you imagine what must have been going on in Simon's mind at that moment?! If there wasn't such a crowd behind him he may have broken the world record for sprinting in the other direction! After all, (Simon must have thought) he was supposed to be on the vacation of a lifetime! He had only wandered over to see what all the fuss was about! Good golly, now the soldier was pressing his spear into his side pushing him forward to take this man's cross!!?!!

Moses just wandered over, curious to see the burning bush that wasn't burning up... then was commissioned to set His people free from the enemy's oppression!! The wisemen just followed the star that had sparked their curiosity... and found the infant Jesus!! Simon just wandered over curious to see what the fuss of the crowd was all about... then was commissioned to carry the cross for Christ!! What fills your heart with wonder and curiosity? The adventure of a life time just might be around the corner, if you're willing to go see, to look up, to find out...

Simon's boys are mentioned here and then Paul writes in Romans 16:13 (NIV) *Greet Rufus, chosen in the Lord, and his mother, who has been a mother to me, too.* It is thought that they became well known in the early church. (How could you not after that experience!?!!) Encounters with Christ will take you well beyond yourself.

Simon was not a random guy in a crowd any more that Moses was just a random shepherd passing by that day. They were chosen. You are chosen. Simon's family was changed the day their father accepted the cross of Christ. You have not passed through this study by chance. You have been invited to go deeper into God's heart through His Word, to carry your cross for Him, to look up and experience the freeing power of the cross He bore for us all. Don't grow weary, for one day you will reap a reward if you do not give up (Gal. 6:9). What has He stirred your curiosity over? Go see dear one, but God Almighty must lead.

What was Jesus offered in Matthew 27:34?

_____

This was probably meant for ridicule as Psalm 69:21 (NIV) states, *They put gall in my food and gave me vinegar for my thirst.* It was also a sedative but Jesus rejected it in order to suffer fully for our sin. *Yet it was the will of the LORD to crush him; he has put him to grief; when his soul makes an offering for guilt, he shall see his offspring; he shall prolong his days; the will of the LORD shall prosper in his hand.* Isaiah 53:10 (ESV)

Jesus had set His focus on His mission. John 18:11 (NIV) *Jesus commanded Peter, "Put your sword away! Shall I not drink the cup the Father has given me?"*

Jesus was not willing to allow the world to numb Him out of His purpose. Have you allowed the world in some way to numb you from your God given purpose or mission? With a breath in our lungs it's still not too late to put away, to reject the cup of the world and receive our fill of the living water of Christ.

We continue to see the Old Testament prophecy fulfilled. Compare Psalm 22:18 with Matthew 27:35

_____

God was, is and will be a God who attends to the details of your life and mine dear one.

Luke 23:32 paints us a picture. What is it?

_____

Two criminals were crucified on either side of Jesus. Glance back at Mark 10:35-39. ____

James and John asked for the places of honor next to Jesus in His Kingdom and what did Jesus tell them (verse 38)?

_____

(NLT) *...Are you able to drink from the bitter cup of suffering I am about to drink?...*

Here as Jesus was preparing to come into His Kingdom the people on His right and left were dying. The way to the Kingdom is to die to self and to live for Christ. The way is through the cross. We forgo our selfish living to live for Christ, to glorify the One who gave His all for us all; to glorify the One who made a way by becoming The Way. Then Jesus said to his disciples, *"Whoever wants to be my disciple must deny themselves and take up their cross and follow me.* Matthew 16:24 (NIV)

Please read Matthew 10:35-38. ____
(Verse 38 NIV) *Whoever does not take up their cross and follow me is not worthy of me.*

There once was a girl named Abigail who saved the day. How did she do it? She died to self and lived for God.

And she rose and bowed with her face to the ground and said, "Behold, your handmaid is a servant to wash the feet of the servants of my lord." 1 Samuel 25:41 (ESV)

We each have a choice. Pilate washed his hands in a bowl of water literally trying to wash his hands of Jesus (Matthew 27:24)… Jesus poured water in a basin, got down and washed people's feet to the glory of His Father (John 13:5). What will you do with the cup you've been handed?

Therefore humble yourselves under the mighty hand of God, that He may exalt you in due time, casting all your care upon Him, for He cares for you. 1 Peter 5:6-7 (NKJV) *...as it is written: "What no eye has seen, what no ear has heard, and what no human mind has conceived" -- the things God has prepared for those who love him--* 1 Corinthians 2:9 (NIV)

You prepare a feast for me in the presence of my enemies. You honor me by anointing my head with oil. My cup overflows with blessings. Psalm 23:5 (NLT)

Thank you for sharing your time with me today, may your cup runneth over in blessings~

Please record what you would like to remember most from today's study.

_____
_____
_____
_____

Day 2: A Way Back In

Hello dear one, welcome back! There really is nothing like God's welcoming wake up call in Lamentations 3:22-23 (NIV) *Because of the LORD's great love we are not consumed, for his compassions never fail. They are new every morning; great is your faithfulness.* EVERY morning, GREAT is His faithfulness! Not just some mornings, EVERY morning! I pray this Truth washes over you afresh and you feel His welcome as you take the playing field of life to begin anew each day.

We have important things to cover today so let's begin in prayer and jump right in.

Please meet me on the other side of Matthew 27:35-56 _____, Mark 15:24-41 _____, Luke 23:33-49 _____ and John 19:18-37. _____ We will take the next two days to dig through these passages so please take your time.

Crucifixion was a slow, torturous and most horrific way to die. In this instance the bodies needed to be buried before sunset due to the Sabbath.

Jesus is now on the cross and we hear an "if… then…" statement we may be all too familiar with. In Matthew 27:40 we see the crowd yelling at Jesus something like, if you are God - then save yourself and come down. This taunt resembles that of the enemy back in Matthew 4:1-11 at the beginning of Jesus' ministry. Just after His baptism the enemy tempted Jesus in the desert with similar statements to prove He was God and could do what He wanted. Luke 4:13 finishes, stating that the devil left Him until another opportune time. What more opportune time then while He's hanging on the cross!

Such it is with us, oftentimes the enemy will come at us when we are in a weak moment or season in life. Weak seasons can come both when things are going really, really bad OR when they are going really, really well. Anytime we take our focus off God it becomes an opportune time for the enemy to strike. Oh, He will strike even when we are focusing on God but his tactics won't be near as successful when our focus is steadfast on our Stronghold

Psalm 27:1 (NIV) *The Lord is my light and my salvation - whom shall I fear? The Lord is the stronghold of my life- of whom shall I be afraid?*

When the crowd made their if/then accusatory statement, rather ironically, because since He WAS God and IS a good, good God, He would not come down - He chose to save us not Himself. The next time we have an, "if God… than why?" scenario running through our head, might we remember the cross. Our "why?" is answered not in "if" but "is". He IS God, so He knows things we don't and understands things we can't, He already gave His life, proving His unfathomable love for us all and so that our circumstance would not end in defeat if we are in Him. We must choose to see our circumstance in faith, set with the backdrop of the cross.

Another jab comes in Matthew 27:43 (NLT). *He trusted God, so let God rescue him now if he wants him! For he said, 'I am the Son of God.'"* Another tactic of the enemy is to get us to doubt our trust placement and the love of our God towards us. God was working out His great and glorious plan in the midst of what appeared to be defeat! In Jesus you ARE a beloved child of God (Galatians 3:26)!! Don't let the enemy deceive you into doubting that! God warned us this world is broken but to take heart He has overcome (John 16:33) and those who endure will arrive safely in His Kingdom (1 Tim. 4:18). (That doesn't guarantee a smooth flight, just a safe landing. So don't jump ship!!)

Nahum 1:7 (NIV) *The Lord is good, a refuge in times of trouble. He cares for those who trust in him,*

In John 19:19 what did the sign say that was hung up on the cross?

_____

From all outward appearances it would seem a mockery however it could not have been more true. Jesus who turns the world's wisdom upside down was indeed coming into His Kingdom and the fact that verse 20 tells us it was stated in three languages declares Jesus is Lord of ALL!

1 Corinthians 1:27 *But God chose the foolish things of the world the shame the wise; God chose the weak things of the world to shame the strong.*

We see redemption and restoration taking place even as Jesus is dying.

Briefly describe the scene in Luke 23:39-43.

_____

_____

Our deeds don't save us, our faith does, and that is a gift of God (Ephesians 2:8). The criminal asked to be remembered… Jesus gave him Paradise! Amazing grace!!

Please describe the scene in John 19:25-27.

_____

_____

To this day family, relationships that last, will be those that are formed at the foot of the cross and remain there acknowledging that apart from Him there is no good thing. Psalm 16:2 (NIV) *I say to the LORD, "You are my Lord; apart from you I have no good thing."*

How do you make an effort to bring your relationships or keep your relationships at the foot of the cross?

_____

Luke 23:44 tells us at about noon when the sun would have been at its highest and brightest what happens?

A symbol of sorrow and God's judgment. See Psalm 23:4 and Isaiah 8:22.

But... Isaiah 9:2 *The people walking in darkness have seen a great light; on those living in the land of deep darkness a light has dawned.* Oh dear one, have you experienced the Light of His love?!

Luke 23:45 tells us what was torn?

With three parts making up the Temple: the courts for all people, the Holy Place for priests and the Most Holy Place where the high priest could enter once a year to atone for the sins of the people. In this Most Holy Place the Ark of the Covenant and God's Presence resided. It was the vail that closed off the Most Holy Place from everything else. That was torn! Matthew's gospel indicates this veil was torn top to bottom - clearly God did the tearing! (Matthew 27:51)

Glance at Genesis 3:24. What did God put in place to block the way into the Garden of Eden after Adam and Eve sinned?

Cherubim and a flaming sword.

Now glance at Exodus 26:31. What did God instruct the people to weave into the intricate design of the curtain separating the Most Holy place from the rest of the Tabernacle?

Do you see a correlation between what blocked the Garden of Eden and the design on the curtain that blocked the entrance to the Most Holy Place? Both had cherubim! The way into His presence was blocked due to the issue of our sin. However Jesus became the Way back into the paradise of His presence through His sacrifice in our place on the cross for the forgiveness of our sin!! The "Do Not Enter" sign was torn because Jesus was willing to become our Way back in! Oh Praise His victorious name!!

When Jesus sacrificed Himself He became the Way! The barrier between God and us was destroyed!! Please take a moment to read Hebrews 9:1-14____ and 10:19-22____.

I will put my laws in their hearts, and I will write them on their minds." Hebrews 10:16 (NIV) It doesn't get more intimate than that!! Arc you allowing Him to write on the tablet of your mind and heart His life changing Truth? How? And are you living like you BELIEVE it's reality? How?

Please take some time to record what God impacted your heart with the deepest through your time in His Word today.

Day 3: "It Is Finished!"

Hello! As promised we are taking a second day to look back at the following passages we began in yesterday. Please begin in prayer as we bow before His leadership and then briefly review and refresh your mind on our Scriptures from yesterday. Matthew 27:35-56 _____, Mark 15:24-41 _____, Luke 23:33-49 _____ and John 19:18-37. _____

Psalm 18:7 (NIV) states, *The earth trembled and quaked, and the foundations of the mountains shook; they trembled because he was angry.* How do you see this verse relate to the evidence Matthew 27:51 gives that the earth shook and the rocks split?

_____

What else did this earthquake cause to open up?

_____

Tombs! In Matthew 27:52-53 what is described?

_____

_____

Verse 53 states, *They came out of the tombs AFTER Jesus' resurrection* (emphasis mine) because what do the following Scriptures tell us about Jesus? 1 Corinthians 15:20-23, and Colossians 1:18.

_____

_____

Firstfruits - Because Jesus lives, we live. He rose first so that we can.

Miraculous events surrounded the event of Jesus' crucifixion: darkness at noon, the tearing of the curtain top to bottom in the Temple, an earthquake and the rising of dead from their tombs!! This was an event that got everyone's attention! There was no question something extremely significant had happened.

From the cross we can glean 7 statements Jesus gives. Speaking would have been near impossible as was breathing so let's not miss what took grave effort to produce. Please look up the following statements and record them.

Luke 23:34

_____

Luke 23:43

_____

John 19:26-27

_____

Matthew 27:46

_____

(Isaiah 53:11, 2 Cor. 5:21, 1 Peter 2:24 - Scripture repeatedly speaks of this event.)

John 19:28

_____

John 19:30

_____

IT IS FINISHED! So why do we often try so hard to earn what has already been fully accomplished for us? Galatians 3:3 (NIV) *Are you so foolish? After beginning by means of the Spirit, are you now trying to finish by means of the flesh?* By faith alone in Jesus we are saved.

Luke 23:46

_____

Through the death of His Son Jesus we now have access to the Father. (Hebrews 10:19)

Do you feel the love dear one? Galatians 2:20 (NIV) ...*I live by faith in the Son of God, who loved me and gave himself for me.*

It is finished. RECEIVE His lavish love and live in His victory!

Please record that which you want to remember most from today's study.

_____

_____

_____

_____

Day 4: Gather Up Courage

Hello friend, welcome! There is the most beautiful row of tulips in my neighborhood and it is one of my favorite places to walk by and savor the message I receive there. You see, these tulips rise up every year in the spring on God's perfect timetable. Not only is that a miracle but the entire row grows up between a long wooden fence line and a rock bed!! Proof that God still grows living hope between a rock and a hard place! As we begin, let's thank Him for being a God of the impossible and bow to His headship in our study.

Yesterday we walked through the crucifixion of Jesus. Briefly describe the event in John 19:31-37.

_____

_____

Where is blood produced? IN THE BONES!! Jesus' bones were never broken (again a fulfillment of Scripture. See Psalm 34:20) thus symbolizing the supply of His sacrificial blood does not run out or short! There is nothing so far gone, no wound or sin so deep that His redeeming blood cannot reach, restore and make new!

Glance back at John 19:29. What type of branch was used to try and reach up and offer Jesus a drink?

_____

Hyssop! The same bush used to wipe the lambs blood over the doorposts in Egypt during the first passover to escape the angel of death!! (Ex. 12:22)

What two things flowed from Jesus when His side was pierced (Jn. 19:34)?

_____

Blood and Water.

His blood poured out with water. Some say that literally Jesus died of a broken heart, a ruptured heart. Blood and water are fluids present in a birth - just as the first bride was taken from or birthed out of the side of the first Adam (See Gen. 2:22), the bride of Christ, the church was born from the side of the last Adam (See 1 Corinthians 15:45). Water and the blood spilled out to make a Way into new life for us. Revelation 1:5 (NIV) …*To him who loves us and has freed us from our sins by his blood,*

Saturated in that hope, please meet me on the other side of Mark 15:42-47 _____, Luke 23:50-56 _____, John 19:38-42 _____ and Matthew 27:57-61. _____ Again we will be taking two days to really dig into these Scripture so please take your time to really savor the blessing of them.

What does Mark 15:43 say about Joseph of Arimathea?

_____

The man took a risk (NLT), *he gathered up courage* (NASB)! I love that! Tell about a time you had to gather up courage to take a risk.

_____

_____

What risk did Joseph take for Jesus?

_____

Joseph was a member of the high counsel and an unknown disciple of Jesus. So that Jesus' body would not be left he requested to take it to his family's tomb, never yet used, carved out of rock. Carved out of what? ROCK! Hold this thought for a bit and we will come back to it.

The Sabbath began at sundown on Friday and ended sundown on Saturday. Jesus died a few hours before sundown on Friday so action had to be taken quickly as no work could be done on the Sabbath. Joseph had to summon up the courage quickly.

I like to call that the 30 second window of courage. Sometimes you just need 30 seconds of bravery to take that first step and the ball begins to roll. So the next time you need some courage don't think about how much you will need to complete the task, rather think to yourself, "I need only 30 seconds of bravery to get me through the first step." Trust God to show up faithful in your obedient first step as you take it knowing He will supply all the rest of the courage and ability you need to proceed as you need it. (See Phil. 2:13, Col. 1:29, Phil. 4:19, Deut. 31:6)

In Mark 15:47 who stood there watching over the action taken with Jesus' body?

_____

Women were not allowed much power or influence in that day and they themselves could not overpower mad crowds. BUT… these women did what they could! They stayed. They courageously stayed present and near Jesus when so many had fled in fear. We will see soon in our study that these women will be the first to witness Jesus' resurrection. God saw they used the opportunities they did have, to honor Him. God honors those who honor Him (1 Sam. 2:30) and He blessed their faithfulness.

What can we do with the opportunities we do have to honor God? Are we making the most of what we can do or are we complaining or worrying about all that we can't?

_____

_____

John's gospel (19:39) indicates there was another brave yet secret disciple of Jesus that helped out Joseph. Who was he?

_____

Nicodemus. Both were afraid to make public their devotion to Jesus because of their high public standing in the community. But in the end we see them step out and take a courageous risk for their God.

Does your community, friends, workplace know where you stand in Christ? Don't be a secret believer, now is the time to step out of hiding for the One who stepped up for you, and let His Light in you shine out to His glory and praise!

Matthew 5:16 (NIV) *In the same way, let your light shine before others, that they may see your good deeds and gorily your Father in heaven.*

We were never meant to compartmentalize our relationship with our God but rather to allow Him to saturate our entire being, all the time, everywhere we go!

Gather courage and act. This world needs the Hope you have!

Please record what has impacted your heart the most today.

_____

_____

_____

_____

Day 5: Out Of Rock

Hello and welcome back my friend. I'm so glad you are here. Do you remember those tulips I told you about that grow from a rock and a hard place near my home? Well today we are going to study how our God has brought Living Hope to every impossible hard spot we may ever find ourselves in!

After praying please review your passages from yesterday to refresh your mind for todays study. Mark 15:42-47 _____, Luke 23:50-56 _____, John 19:38-42 _____ and Matthew 27:57-61. _____

How many pounds of spice did they bring to treat Jesus' body according to John 19:39?

_____

75 POUNDS! There was no hiding their devotion now! This amount was spice enough for royalty!

According to Matthew 27:60 they laid Jesus in a tomb carved out of rock and then what was rolled across the front?

_____

A GREAT stone. My NLT doesn't just say stone but a GREAT stone! What was done in addition to the tomb according to verse 65-66?

_____

Jesus is placed in stone, covered by a GREAT stone, sealed shut and guarded. Seems this trial, this hardship is impossible. Our Hope was caught between a rock and a hard place.

Have you ever felt like your hope in a particular situation was caught between a rock and a hard place?

_____

If you have traveled with us since "Trust in The Light" remember back to the beginning when Mary was faced with the impossible (Luke 1:34) and what was she told? See Luke 1:37.

_____

For nothing will be impossible with God." (ESV)

When you have tried all in your trial, made the most of every opportunity and done all that you could… trust Him to be Who He is… the God of the impossible.

Joshua won a battle by walking around a building.
Jehoshaphat won a battle through praise.
Gideon won a battle with clay pots.
Moses escaped the enemy through the Red Sea on dry ground.
David killed a giant with a river stone.
Sarah had a baby in her 90's.

Ezekiel saw dry bones come to life as an army.

This is only "how" they got through their battle not "why". They never in their wildest dreams could have even suggested to God the battle plans He provided! However they TRUSTED His Way, His perspective, His timing, His choice and they didn't give up but walked it out in obedient dependence on Him through trust by faith.

Sometimes that plan God provides requires a walk with Him called "wait". This might be among the toughest battle plans around! But when our Living Hope seemed to be caught in between a rock and a hard place with no way of escape what was required for three days? Nothing. We had to wait. Then like my tulips… carved out of the sheer rock of impossibility, walked our Rock! Beauty from ashes, Living Hope!

When you have tried all in your trial, trust the One who finished His work on the cross so that the work He's started in you can be carried on to a glorious completion. For nothing, no, nothing is impossible for our God!

Yet the LORD longs to be gracious to you; therefore he will rise up to show you compassion. For the LORD is a God of justice. Blessed are all who wait for him! Isaiah 30:18 (NIV)

Out from behind the rock of impossibility came our Rock of stability, trust Him.

You will keep in perfect peace whose mind is stayed on you, because he trusts in you. Trust in the LORD forever, for the LORD GOD is an everlasting rock. Isaiah 26:3-4 (ESV) The rendition of these verses found in the Message Bible goes like this… *People with their minds set on you, you keep completely whole, steady on their feet, because they keep at it and don't quit. Depend on GOD and keep at it because in the LORD GOD you have a sure thing.*

from the end of the earth I call to you when my heart is faint. Lead me to the rock that is higher than I, Psalm 61:2 (ESV)

Please record what you want to remember most from today's study.

_____

_____

_____

_____

God bless you muchly dear one~

Day 6 & 7: A Time To Reflect

Over the next two days take time to reflect over your week of study. Maybe you need some time to catch up on the study material and this might be the perfect break to do just that with the Lord!

I encourage you to glance back at the final point at the end of each day that you recorded having had the greatest impact on your heart. As you spend time with God in prayer, reflect and record on the lines below how God is tying it all together and applying it to your life.

Ask that God make it clear who He would have you invite into a natural opportunity to share Him, to apply what you are learning. Trust Him to continue to take the lead. May we have a heart ever ready with eyes and ears out to the opportunities God wants to invite us into for His glory and praise.

Do not merely listen to the word, and so deceive yourselves. Do what it says. Anyone who listens to the word but does not do what it says is like someone who looks at his face in a mirror and, after looking at himself, goes away and immediately forgets what he looks like.

But whoever looks intently into the perfect law that gives freedom, and continues in it - not forgetting what they have heard, but doing it - they will be blessed in what they do. James 1:22-25 (NIV)

_____

_____

_____

_____

_____

Philippians 4:13 (NIV) *I can do all things through him who gives me strength.*

John 14:26 (NIV) *But the Advocate, the Holy Spirit, whom the Father will send in my name, will teach you all things and will remind you of everything I have said to you.*

WEEK 8

...victory rests with the Lord. Proverbs 21:32 (NIV)

Day 1: Just As He Said

Welcome back my friend. Thank you so much for your enduring tenacity to finish strong! He who promised is faithful and will honor your faithfulness to Him. Let's bow in prayer that we allow Him His rightful place as Lead in our study today.

Please meet me on the other side of Matthew 28:1-15 ____, Mark 16:1-11 ____, Luke 24:1-12 ____ and John 20:1-18. ____ These Scriptures are packed full of wonderful Truths so we will be taking today and tomorrow to fully digest these portions of Scripture.

When Jesus rose early on the first day of the week, he appeared first to Mary Magdalene, out of whom he had driven seven demons. Mark 16:9 (NIV)

Of all the people Jesus could have appeared to first after He resurrects why do you think He chose Mary Magdalene?

_____

Off the bat I see two factors that would have disqualified her as a worthy contender for an opportunity like that based on the worlds standards. For starters she was a woman and not just any woman but a woman with a pretty shady past! Praise God He doesn't judge us according to worldly standards.

Jesus saw a gal with a heart so captivated by His love that she had rooted herself back at the last place she had encountered Him, desperate for Truth. Jesus saw a girl forgiven and set free from much and therefore loved Him much. Luke 7:47 (NLT) *"I tell you, her sins—and they are many—have been forgiven, so she has shown me much love. But a person who is forgiven little shows only little love."*

Mary Magdalene loved much and went back to what she knew and found her faith for all that she didn't. *Indeed, if you call out for insight and cry aloud for understanding, and if you look for it as for silver and search for it as for hidden treasure, then you will understand the fear of the LORD and find the knowledge of God.* Proverbs 2:3-5 (NIV) *...the LORD has compassion on those who fear him;* Psalm 103:13 (NIV)

Each gospel account that you just read as we started today makes note that it was very early in the morning that these women set out to tend to the body of Jesus. Who now is considered the body of Christ?

_____

The Church! The church body is the bride of Christ! So how are we motivated to get up early and tend the needs of others?

Mark 16:3 tells us these women really were unsure exactly how they were going to go about caring for Jesus. On the way it states they were discussing their concerns among themselves. In thinking on how we might show our care and love for Jesus let's remember back to the two greatest commandments in Mark 12:29-31 (NIV) *"The most important one," answered Jesus, "is this: 'Hear, O Israel: The Lord our God, the Lord is one. Love the Lord your God with all your heart and with all your soul and with all your mind and with all your strength.' The second is this: 'Love your neighbor as yourself.' There is no commandment greater than these."*

You can't love God with your whole being and not love your neighbor because the way we show our love for God is to love one another!

John 13:35 (NIV) *By this everyone will know that you are my disciples, if you love one another."*

In Luke 10:25-37 an expert in the law asks Jesus who is this "neighbor" we are to love like ourselves?! Jesus answers his question with a parable that explains how to be neighborly. It's quite possible if I concern myself more with being neighborly my "neighbor" will just show up.

How have you been given the chance to exemplify your love for Christ by being neighborly?

What specifically weighed on the hearts of these women as they walked on toward the tomb? (Mark 16:3)

Who would roll that stone away?! They were up against impossible obstacles and yet they still got up early and pursued their God given purpose!! What have you pursued, maybe even against impossible obstacles, urged on by sheer gratitude for His incomprehensible and lavish love for you?

As they walked on in faith what did these women look up to find in Mark 16:4?

They looked up and found God Almighty had already taken care of their impossibilities!! Sometimes He takes away the obstacle in our way and sometimes He leaves it so that we will depend on Him, lean into Him, so that He can help us shoulder the weight of it, proving that in our weakness He indeed is strong!

Paul, in 2 Corinthians battled a thorn that God allowed to remain. As much as it pains God to leave a thorn it would pain Him more to lose our heart due to the pride that would fill the gap of that "healed" wound. Sometimes a thorn is left to prevent the formation of a stumbling block to an intimate relationship with Him.

No suffering will outweigh His sufficient grace to withstand the weight of it.

2 Corinthians 12:9 (NIV) *But he said to me, "My grace is sufficient for you, for my power is made perfect in weakness." Therefore I will boast all the more gladly about my weaknesses, so that Christ's power may rest on me.*

The angels at the tomb ask the women a question. According to Luke 24:5 what is it?

_____

Why are you looking for the living among the dead?! Might we check ourselves with this question too? Do we expect to find God moving in our church, situation, relationships, workplace, trials?! John 5:17 tells us He is ALWAYS working so how do you seek our LIVING, working God in possibly dead situations? How big are your expectations for Him to do exceedingly and abundantly more than you could ask or imagine?! Nothing stays dead in His life giving hand.

In Mark 16:7 who is singled out in the message given to these women to carry?

_____

Peter! Now considering all that Peter went through with the denials and the rooster crowing at Jesus' death, why do you think the angels would specify to tell His disciples, INCLUDING PETER?

_____

Peter like Mary Magdalene needed to hear that His power had indeed overcome even this; Jesus is our eternal Living Hope.

Now in Luke 24:10-12 with everyone in disbelief who is it that runs to the tomb to verify the ladies report?

_____

PETER! This dear man like Mary Magdalene, needed the story not to be dead! We all needed The Story not to be dead because that means our story has not died!!! No matter what pit your story had been drug through, our God is RISEN, He LIVES and thus so can YOU! We do not end in defeat but victory as a believer in Jesus Christ as our Savior!!

The Resurrection is so very important as it confirms our world is headed for redemption not disaster! Death has been conquered and thus we have eternal life! Our Savior lives which gives authority to the church's witness to the world, there is meaning in the act of communion, we can find meaning even in tragedy, and His resurrection assures us of Living Hope! We are not left powerless in this broken world but have the power that raised Jesus from the dead living in us by way of the Holy Spirit!

1 Corinthians 15:51, 43 (NLT) *But let me reveal to you a wonderful secret. We will not all die, but we will all be transformed! (43) Our bodies are buried in brokenness, but they will be raised in glory. They are buried in weakness, but they will be raised in strength.*

RAISED IN GLORY AND STRENGTH!! Hallelujah!! Praise our Victorious One!!

Mark 16:7 (NLT) *...Jesus is going ahead of you to Galilee. You will see him there, just as he told you before he died."*

Please underline "just as he told you" in the above verse. We will always find things just as He has told us. Every word of God is flawless (Proverbs 30:5). Oftentimes He doesn't give us the details to His step by step schedule but that doesn't mean He doesn't have one. Like Hannah in 1 Samuel waited for the birth of her promised son that may not have occurred on her timetable but rather, *...in the course of time...* 1 Samuel 1:20 (NIV). In the course of His perfect timing Hannah did conceive.

God will bring to conception His perfect plan for our lives in His perfect timing if we will only abide in Him while we wait. In our wait we can rest in that we know WHO holds the plan and by WHAT power it will be brought about in us, the HOW of the Holy Spirit. The actual WHEN is within really the only mighty hands that can handle such details.

Today let's surrender our "WHEN's?!" As we choose to rest in the victory of knowing our WHO, WHAT, and HOW! *"Don't let your hearts be troubled. Trust in God,…* John 14:1 (NLT) *That is why I am suffering as I am. Yet this is no cause for shame, because I know whom I have believed, and am convinced that he is able to guard what I have entrusted to him until that day.* 2 Timothy 1:12 (NIV)

Let us pause here and record the greatest point of impact made on your heart today.

_____
_____
_____
_____

Day 2: Sometimes We Just Need To Do It Afraid

Welcome back my friend! As promised we will be picking up right back in the same group of passages we started in yesterday. Please pray and then refresh your mind in those Scriptures for todays context. Matthew 28:1-15 ____, Mark 16:1-11 ____, Luke 24:1-12 ____ and John 20:1-18. ____

Jumping right back in where we left off yesterday… what town is mentioned in Mark 16:7 that Jesus was on going ahead to meet them in?

_____

Galilee. Anywhere Jesus asks us to go we can be sure He will go ahead of us. Deuteronomy 31:8 (NIV) *The LORD himself goes before you and will be with you; he will never leave you nor forsake you. Do not be afraid; do not be discouraged."*

Interestingly enough, although Jesus had said to meet Him in Galilee it seems in fear they have locked themselves in Jerusalem so Jesus meets them there and then later in Galilee. (John 20:19, Luke 24:36, John 21) Praise God He meets us right where we are at and grows us up from there!

According to Matthew 28:8, what two emotions did these women leave the tomb with?

_____

The NLT gives us, very frightened and filled with great joy!?!! When was the last time you were very frightened and yet filled with great joy?!! In spite of the swirling emotions within, they set out resolutely on the mission with the message God had entrusted them with and wouldn't you know it… in verse 9 NLT *And as they went, Jesus met them and greeted them*…. It was on the way that Jesus met them!!! Ever faithful! So often we wait for verification or the subsiding of fear before we proceed into our calling. Sometimes that is what is required however there are times we need to just step in faith and He is faithful to meet us AS we go and walk out that which He has asked of us. Sometimes we just need to do it afraid.

Exodus 14:15 (NIV) finds Moses in just such a situation as he faced the Red Sea before him and the enemy in pursuit behind him. Moses needed to just move forward. *Then the LORD said to Moses, "Why are you crying out to me? Tell the Israelites to move on.* When you have sought the Lord and you know what He wants you to do don't let fear hold you back He will be there AS you go - TRUST.

Joshua 3:13 (NIV) paints for us a similar picture, here Joshua is to cross the Jordan. The priests needed to step in first before the water would part. *And as soon as the priests who carry the ark of the LORD--the Lord of all the earth--set foot in the Jordan, its waters flowing downstream will be cut off and sand up in a heap."* TRUST.

It's often as you go, as you walk out your faith that you find Him to be more than you ever could have imagined.

Do you have an area you feel God calling you out past your fear? How can you take hold of His courage and in God-confidence walk out in Him?

_____

_____

I truly love John's inclusion of the details surrounding Mary's encounter with Jesus outside the tomb in John 20:11-18.

In verse 13 (NLT) she is in a state of distress, crying. *"Dear woman, why are you crying?" the angels asked her. "Because they have taken away my Lord," she replied, "and I don't know where they have put him."* Underline "they have taken: and "I don't know" in that verse.

I'm sure we could relate on some level to her emotional state. And verse 14 tells us Jesus was right there in the cloud of her sad confusion, He was with her even there. But she didn't realize it, she didn't recognize Him. She mistakes Him for the gardener in verse 15! Maybe He has shown up in our "cloud" and we just have not recognized His presence? Maybe our own expectations as to how we think He should show up (like expecting a gardener) is what is clouding our vision of His better way?

But blessed are your eyes because they see, and your ears because they hear. Matthew 13:16 (NIV) I pray for these perceptive eyes and ears.

In John 20:16 we find Jesus calling her by name and then she does see and she does hear Truth!!

"Do not fear, for I have redeemed you; I have summoned you by name; you are mine. Isaiah 43:1 (NIV) Do you hear Him calling you? Because He is, dear one, He most certainly is.

Even the great apostle Paul couldn't hardly believe the goodness of God to call even him! 1 Corinthians 15:9-10 (NLT) *For I am the least of all the apostles. In fact, I'm not even worthy to be called an apostle after the way I persecuted God's church. But whatever I am now, it is all because God poured out his special favor on me - and not without results….* He didn't take it for granted that God had called him by name but responded by sharing the love God poured out in his heart, with His church.

Matthew 28:11-15 tells us of a conspiracy contrived to counteract the Truth, however it probably was not circulated until the Truth of His resurrection came out! We can almost count on the moment we step out into the Truth He has spoken over us we will be combated by lies and discouragement as well. The enemy is prowling around like a roaring lion just waiting for someone to devour so be alert and sober minded (1 Peter 5:8)!

Back it up to Matthew 28:10. How does Jesus address the ones who deserted Him at His death?!

Brothers!!! Jesus said, Go tell my brothers…! The denial and rejection was still a fresh wound only committed a short three days ago and yet the wounds in his feet and hands ran much deeper. So deep there is no wound that His healing, restoration can not run deeper still!

Before we close today let's look at one more point in John 20 we surely do not want to miss made in verse 7. How was the cloth left that had been wrapped around Jesus' head?

FOLDED!! That doesn't sound like a grave robbery to me!!

"Do not let your hearts be troubled. You believe in God; believe also in me. My Father's house has many rooms; if that were not so, would I have told you that I am going there to prepare a place for you? And if I go and prepare a place for you, I will come back and take you to be with me that you also may be were I am. You know the way to the place where I am going." John 14:2-4 (NIV)

Jesus answered, "I am the way and the truth and the life. No one comes to the Father except through me. John 14:6 (NIV)

Peace I leave with you; my peace I give you. I do not give to you as the world gives. Do not let your hearts be troubled and do not be afraid. John 14:27 (NIV)

For it will be just as He has said dear one… *The LORD Almighty has sworn, "Surely, as I have planned, so it will be, and as I have purposed, so it will happen.* Isaiah 14:24 (NIV)

Faith over fear.

Please record that which you would like to remember most from today's study.

Day 3: Cleopas - Glory To The Father!

Hello, thank you for your return! Has not the continued return of each other's fellowship in the Word stirred up the motivation to continue! The sureness of our God's return for us stirs quite a motivation within to bring glory to our Father while we wait!! Bow with me in prayer as we proceed into the depths of His wonderful Truth.

Please read Mark 16:12-13 _____ as well as a much more detailed account of this encounter is found in Luke 24:13-35. _____

The encounter in Mark is recorded briefly in that two left the city and upon an encounter with Jesus were found rushing back into the city! Can you recount an encounter with Jesus, maybe in your study, prayer time or in His Word that sent your heart rushing, wanting to share what God had done or communicated to you?

_____

_____

But if I say, "I will not mention his word or speak anymore in his name," his word is in my heart like a fire, a fire shut up in my bones. I am weary of holding it in; indeed, I cannot. Jeremiah 20:9 (NIV)

Where were the two followers of Jesus traveling to, in Luke 24:13?

_____

Emmaus. Which means warm spring. Keep this in mind as we study today and we will circle back around to it.

Luke 24 verses 14 and 15 start out in the NLT, (14) *As they walked...* and (15) *As they talked...* so as these men were in motion verse 15 tells us Jesus Himself suddenly came and began walking with them!!! Are you willing to make room in your motion filled moments to receive an encounter with Jesus?

The Scripture tells us these men did not recognize Him. What does Jesus ask them in Luke 24:17?

_____

Jesus is God and already knew what they were talking about so why do you think He asks them?

_____

I think He wanted to walk with them, He wanted their companionship and to have them share their hearts with Him. It's one thing to know what your child or even a friend is feeling but another thing altogether for them to call on you wanting to willingly share their heart just because they want your companionship and to spend some time with you. Recall a time when someone was willing to share their heart with you. How did that make you feel?

_____

Now imagine how God the Father who knit your very heart together feels when you want to share it back with Him!

These men responded to the presence of Jesus. Though they did not know it was Jesus they did not shun a stranger but welcomed Him on their journey and into their conversation. Hebrews 13:2 (NIV) *Do not forget to show hospitality to strangers, for by so doing some people have shown hospitality to angels without knowing it.*

In the NLT Luke 24 verses 17 and 18 read this way; ...*They stopped short, sadness written across their faces. Then one of them, Cleopas, replied, "You must be the only person in Jerusalem who hasn't heard about all the things that have happened there the last few days."* Now considering the current events of their times they were probably not exaggerating their feelings however, your's truly, can relate on some level to being tempted (just a bit) to being over dramatic at times! Who am I kidding? Not just tempted I dare say I HAVE been over dramatic and not just a bit! But what does Jesus do with their dramatic reply (even if their drama is verifiable)? (Verse 19)

He encourages them to tell Him more. We won't find a better listener than God Himself.

1 Peter 5:7 (NIV) *Cast all your anxiety on him because he cares for you.* That verse says ALL not some, but all your cares, all your anxieties, why? Because He cares!!! He cares! He doesn't get worn out or bogged down or too tired, He is the great I Am all that you need!

How have you exercised your free access to the Great Counselor (Is. 9:6)?

In Luke 24:21 (NLT) we clearly hear dashed hope. *"We had hoped…"* hoped, past tense. And *"this all happened three days ago."* like even if there had been a little hope, now too much time had lapsed and clearly there was just no possibility of hope left.

As these men continue to relay what they know to Jesus (whom they do not yet know is Jesus) they relay that they were given an AMAZING report from some women just that very morning (verse 22)! So why were they not happy?

Being given the gift of Truth and actually receiving it are two very different things. How would you explain the difference between being given a gift and actually receiving one?

When these two men finish casting their cares, Jesus makes His response. Isaiah 65:24 (NIV) states, *Before they call I will answer; while they are still speaking I will hear.* Amazing! He is always ahead of us! We just don't want to miss His answer because it wasn't what we expected. We can trust Him to be exceedingly more than we could have imagined as we allow Him to frame our new perspective.

Read Isaiah 1:15-18 and record what might hinder our prayers from being heard? And how might we have control of fixing this dilemma?

_____

_____

Sin can create a barrier but that wall is one wrecking ball prayer away if we sincerely confess our sin. He then is faithful and just to forgive us and then the conduit is clean and clear (1 John 1:9)! Praise Him!

In our passage in Luke we see Jesus respond immediately to these two men. In Luke 24:25-27 what does Jesus point them to in order to dispel their confusion and despair?

_____

_____

The Scriptures of course!! Look one more time at verse 27. Oh I sure would like to hear that sermon podcast!!! Jesus explained all the Scriptures concerning Himself!! Can you just imagine!?!!

Verse 28 tells me they were nearing Emmaus or "warm spring" and the end of their journey, good thing too because God's about to Isaiah 43:19 (NIV) this whole thing!! *See, I am doing a new thing! Now it springs up; do you not perceive it? I am making a way in the wilderness and streams in the wasteland.*

Is it gettin' warm in here to you too or what?! We are nearing the "warm spring", Emmaus and Jesus is about to reveal to them who He is and that He is doing NEW things… streams in the wasteland kind of things!!

Have you ever experienced Him making a way in the wilderness or a stream in the wasteland, so to speak?

_____

_____

In Luke 24:28 Jesus acted like what?

_____

Like He was going on… but what did the men do in verse 29?

_____

They asked Him to stay! Jesus comes into a heart, by invitation.

What happens in Luke 24:30-31?

_____

_____

They commune with Jesus. He breaks the bread with nail scarred hands!! It's at the foot of the cross in communion with our God that things become clear! Jesus is the Lamb that was slain to take away the sin of the world as John the Baptist had proclaimed! His body the true Bread of Life broken to make us whole. He is the Lion of Judah who has risen in victory and now leads us in triumphal procession!!!

These men looked at each other and exclaimed what, in Luke 24:32?

_____

"Didn't our hearts burn within us as he talked with us on the road and explained the Scriptures to us?" (NLT)

"Is not my word like fire," declares the LORD,... Jeremiah 23:29 (NIV)

Never underestimate your God given Spark within... it takes only an amber to start a bonfire!

Speaking of energized hearts these men within the same hour were ready to head back to Jerusalem!! This was no short trip. We are talking 7 miles!! They had just arrived and now they had found a mighty second wind to make a turnaround trek!! When you hear the Word of the Lord and you invite the Bread of Life in and commune with Him it affects life turn around! Life changes with new found energy and zest for the warm spring in the wilderness and fresh streams found where once lay only wasteland!

Who did these men go to when they arrived back in Jerusalem (verse 33)?

_____

The eleven disciples.

What did they tell the disciples in Luke 24:34?

_____

The same amazing report that they had heard that very morning from the women!!! If they had received the gift of Truth the first time it would have saved them a 14 mile trek! What might we avoid by choosing to trust the gift of Truth in all situations the first time around?

Maybe you have learned this lesson the hard way. Remember Jesus still used their 14 mile journey together for good, to teach them and lead them into all Truth. (Romans 8:28) So don't lose heart but lose the ties of lies so that you may receive the Truth that sets one free (and maybe even free yourself from a few rough miles).

Cleopas and his friend rushed back to the glory of the Father to exclaim the Truth of Living Hope!! Cleopas' name means, (get this) "glory to the father"! God used their journey together to ultimately bring glory to the Father and on the road to "warm spring" He revealed He is the spring of Living Water that wells up within a person to eternal life able to melt even the hardest heart if only they will turn to Him and invite Him in.

...Behold, now is the favorable time; behold, now is the day of salvation.
2 Corinthians 6:2 (ESV)

Please record what you would like to remember most from today's study.

_____

_____

_____

_____

Day 4: Without A Doubt

Without a doubt you are welcome here my friend and you are loved. Here is a verse to tuck into the pocket of our hearts as we begin our study in prayer, thanking Him for never leaving our hearts wanting. *For his unfailing love for us is powerful; the LORD's faithfulness endures forever. Praise the LORD!* Psalm 117:2 (NLT)

Please meet me on the other side of Mark 16:14 _____, Luke 24:36-49 _____ and John 20:19-29. _____

Following the two men returning with good news from their journey with Jesus along the road to Emmaus, we enter the scene now in the middle of their great rendition of all that happened! Luke 24:36 (NLT) tells us that, *...just* *as they were telling about it, Jesus himself was suddenly standing there among them....* (Talk about a mic drop moment!!)

Psalm 22:3 tell us our God inhabits our praises! Please read Psalm 150. ____

Seems our baseline for praise is not our circumstance or emotions but rather if we are breathing! We were made to praise the Lord at all times! Seems there really are only two times; when we feel like it and when we don't. So today let's just choose to praise Him always and anyways - especially when we don't feel like it as that is probably when we need to feel His presence most nearly and clearly!!

Luke 24:37 relays the emotional state of the men. What are they feeling?

_____

Startled and frightened. What does Jesus ask in verse 38?

_____

Why are your hearts filled with doubt?

Jesus doesn't wait for a response He rather jumps right in with doubt dispeller! He begins in verse 39 with, "Look..." So He begins with a focus shift. Is there any area in your life that needs a focus shift? Maybe from the mountain to the Mountain Mover?

_____

Why does Isaiah 54:17 tell us that no weapon formed against us will prosper? Well, look one verse back, Isaiah 54:16. Who made the blacksmith that forged the weapon?

_____

God is still above it all dear one! He reigns victorious! Any thing that comes to us must first be sifted through His nail scarred hands. He will only allow what

He can bring about for our good and His glory. Remember when Jesus told Peter, Satan had asked to sift him like wheat in Luke 22:31?! His next sentence (verse 32) was but I have prayed for you… When God Almighty prays for you, you know you'll receive what you need to prevail victoriously against the enemies weapons!

In Luke 24:39 Jesus redirected their focus to what?

_____

Look at My hands, look at My feet. In verse 40 it says He showed them his hands and feet. Look at the cross, abide at the foot of the cross and He will reveal great and unsearchable things you do not know. (Jeremiah 33:3)

Luke 24:41 tells us they still stood there in unbelief however what is their emotional state now?

_____

Joy and wonder! So startled and frightened to joy and wonder just by looking at the cross He carried for us! Things still did not all make sense, but their emotional state was improving!

Luke 24:45 Can be turned into a constant prayer of ours.
"Dear God, please open my mind to understand the Scriptures. In Jesus name, Amen."

The Good News isn't just for us to understand. Who is the Truth intended to reach according to verse 47?

_____

ALL the world!

What did Jesus say He would send in Luke 24:49 to help us and fill us with the power of heaven?

_____

Do we live like we know that we as believers are filled with the power of heaven; His Holy Spirit?! How do we live out this belief in His Truth?

_____

What Truth do you gain confidence from in the following Scriptures?
John 14:16 (NIV) *And I will ask the Father, and he will give you another advocate to help you and be with you forever—* John 14:26 (NIV) *But the Advocate, the Holy Spirit, whom the Father will send in my name, will teach you all things and will remind you of everything I have said to you.* John 16:13 (NIV) *But when he, the Spirit of truth, comes, he will guide you into all truth. He will not speak on his own; he will speak only what he hears, and he will tell you what is yet to come.* and Romans 8:11 (NIV) *And if the Spirit of him who raised Jesus from the dead is living in you, he who raised Christ from the dead will also give life to your mortal bodies because of his Spirit who lives in you.*

_____

What does Mark 16:14 find Jesus rebuking His disciples for?

_____

Stubborn unbelief or hardness of heart. Ezekiel 36:26 (NIV) states, *I will give you a new heart and out a new spirit in you; I will remove from you your heart of stone and give you a heart of flesh.* God can transform a heart but we need to let down our guard and invite Him to do so. On the other side of humility is where wisdom is found. (See Proverbs 11:2.) We have to confess that we don't know it all, that we are not going to know it all this side of heaven and that we need a Savior who is Christ the Lord and begin to Trust the One, the only One with the shoulders strong enough to carry the weight of this broken world.

In John 20 we see that one of the disciples was MIA when Jesus first appeared to the group. Knowing Thomas Jesus knew a second trip would be necessary for Thomas to believe and so Jesus takes that step. He always takes the first step toward us in pursuit of our whole heart. He's the romancer of our souls. *But God demonstrates his own love for us in this: While we were still sinners, Christ died for us.* Romans 5:8 (NIV)

...Don't be faithless any longer. Believe!" John 20:27 (NLT) Jesus exclaims this to Thomas after once again directing his focus to the effects of the cross.

If you have doubt let it deepen your faith as you seek answers. *You will seek me and find me when you seek me with all your heart.* Jeremiah 29:13 (NIV)

Thomas responds with a sincere exclamation of faith in John 20:28. Please record his 5 word response to Jesus below.

_____

"My Lord and my God!" (NIV) One day everyone will acknowledge Him as God. Romans 14:11 (NIV) tells us, *It is written: "'As surely as I live,' says the Lord, 'every knee will bow before me; every tongue will acknowledge God.'"* May we choose to love Him NOW as our personal Lord and Savior God just as Thomas did, before it's too late.

Then Jesus told him, "Because you have seen me, you have believed; blessed are those who have not seen and yet have believed. John 20:29 (NIV)

Please record what really impacted your heart today.

_____
_____
_____
_____

Day 5: Feed My Sheep

Welcome my friend! Today we will savor one of my most favorite portions of Scripture! Well, I have lots of favorite parts in Scripture. I guess basically the whole Bible is my favorite! There is no book like His Living Word, but I don't know, something about our Saviors heart in John chapter 21 just gets me every time! Let's bow before our perfect Savior that He might lead us deeper into His perfect love.

Please meet me now at John 21:1-23. _____

John 21:1 (NLT) *Later, Jesus appeared again to the disciples beside the Sea of Galilee....*

At the tomb he told the women to tell His disciples and Peter to meet Him at Galilee. He would go ahead of them and meet them there just as He had told them before He had died. (Mark 16:7) When Jesus gives us His Word that He will be with us, that He will meet us in that step of faith, His Word can be trusted. How have you experienced Jesus showing up right where He promised He would for you?

_____

_____

The first time He appears to His disciples He does it in Jerusalem because they were too afraid to go to Galilee just yet. (John 20:11-23 after the Emmaus encounter and John 20:26-29 just for Thomas.) Jesus doesn't write them off because of their fear but rather meets them where they are at. Does that touch your heart like it does mine?! Not only that but He came back even for just the one, just as He had preached He would (See Luke 15:1-7.)!

Just as Jesus met the disciples in the middle of the lake when He clearly said He would meet them on the other side indicating they would make it to the outer side (Mark 6:45-52); He knows and sees our need in the middle of our storm and is willing to back track to further embolden our faith as we seek to follow Him faithfully in the journey!

He knows you and sees you, He gives you His faithful Word that you will arrive safely (1 Tim. 4:18) yet He compassionately takes the time to encourage us along the way in our middle steps… too far from shore and too far from the other side… He knows the anxiety that can well up inside almost surpassing the height of the waves in the actual storm!

… *"Be still, and know that I am God;…* Psalm 46:10 (NIV) *…take a new grip with your tired hands and strengthen your weak knees.* Hebrews 12:12 (NLT) … *"Never will I leave you; never will I forsake you."* Hebrews 13:5 (NIV)

Here they are at the Sea of Galilee and if anyone out there is possibly feeling completely worthless after a colossal failure and in need of special encouragement, this chapter is for you dear one.

John 21:4 tells me they couldn't see who He was but they heard His voice. Please record John 10:27 below.

_____

_____

Becoming familiar with someone's voice takes spending time with them. I'm praying this study has helped develop our voice recognition skills! The disciples in Mark 6:30-52 experienced a great miracle of five loaves and two fish feeding 5000!! Yet a moment later they are terrified in a storm because their hearts were too hard! If we will take the time to notice what motivates our Savior's heart, who He is and what He is about, we will be reassured in our storms with the ability to take courage in a trust that trumps all fear! We will notice the tone of His voice as we discover His character through His Word.

John 21:6 indicates success after following a direction that would have appeared futile! "No one" randomly casts a net into the sea and finds success, just as "no one" kills a giant with one river stone (1 Sam. 17) and "no one" parts the Red Sea with a shepherd staff (Ex. 14) or wins a battle by walking around a city 7 times (Josh. 6)… the Bible is filled with successful plans "no one" would have believed possible. However when infused with trust in a faithful God anything becomes possible! What is your impossible possibility?

_____

How do the following Scriptures embolden your faith and trust in the God of the impossible to step out into what may seem futile? Luke 1:37 (NIV) *For no word from God will ever fail."* Isaiah 30:21 (NIV) *Whether you turn to the right or to the left, your ears will hear a voice behind you, saying, "This is the way; walk in it."* Matthew 19:26 (NIV) *Jesus looked at them and said, "With man this is impossible, but with God all things are possible."* Also see 1 Corinthians 1:26-31. ____

_____

_____

Sometimes being called to step into the "waiting room" of life is what seems impossible but if that is where God has called you for a season you can be positive He is with you even there. Every waiting millisecond will be for great purpose too. The Author of time doesn't waste it, even in the waiting room. *Yet the LORD longs to be gracious to you; therefore he will rise up to show you compassion. For the LORD is a God of justice. Blessed are all who wait for him!* Isaiah 30:18 (NIV)

In John 21:9 what did Jesus already have prepared; over what kind of fire?

_____

He had prepared to serve them a breakfast of fish and bread over a charcoal fire!!

First Jesus greets them by doing the same miracle as He did when He first called them. See Luke 5 for the miracle catch of fish and the call to follow Him as He promised to make them fishers of men. After Peter's colossal failure of denying Christ three times he may very well have felt he had failed out of his commission to "fish for men" yet here we see Jesus almost presenting Peter a do over! Even prepping the stage with the same charcoal fire found in John 18:18 that Peter was warming himself by when he made the denials!

Jesus knew how far Peter had fallen and yet here Jesus is pictured serving a meal of fish and bread that once before He miraculously provided to meet a need spaning 5,000+. His provision went well beyond anyone's wildest imaginations (See John 6:1-14.)! Maybe quite possibly Jesus was trying to communicate to Peter that there is no pit of sin His ability to provide forgiveness for does not run deeper still. Our God is a God of the above and beyond what we could every possibly imagine (Eph. 3:20)!!

The stage is set yet one more detail just gets me… Jesus has already prepared breakfast and is in need of nothing yet what does He ask them for in verse 10?

_____

He asks them to bring some of what they have caught!!! He wants what we have to offer even if it is just five loaves and two fish. *"Here is a boy with five small barley loaves and two small fish, but how far will they go among so many?"* John 6:9 (NIV) It seems no one but Jesus truly saw the potential in this boys meager offering of all that he had. Matthew 14:18 (NIV) *"Bring them here to me,"*… Jesus said.

He sees your potential, He sees what only He can do with all the little you have. Trust Him, give it all and tune into His voice alone who took the loaves and gave thanks… He gave thanks!!! He gave thanks for the small which was all that little boy had. When we are willing to trust Him with our "weak" His strong shines even brighter!!! *But we have this treasure in jars of clay to show that this all-surpassing power is from God and not from us.* 2 Corinthians 4:7 (NIV)

Please note the three questions Jesus asks Peter alongside his responses in John 21:15-17. These three questions mirror Peter's three denials.

Peter may have felt he had fallen too far short to still be commissioned by Jesus and yet Jesus goes to great lengths to break through those lies and three times Jesus recommissions Peter! Through Peter's repentance He is reconciled to Christ and recommissioned to feed His lambs, care for and feed His sheep! Jesus did not ask off handedly or haphazardly… He laid down His life for the sheep (including His sheep named Peter and His sheep named (your name) _____) (John 10:11) so Jesus wasn't finding Peter a spot as a last resort… He was entrusting Him with great responsibility because He saw His greatness still living within Peter!!

Understanding the importance of going deeper in a love relationship with God will show itself in the way we love others. Do we understand His love for us in a way that it grows a love in our hearts back for Him? How does your knowledge of Christ's deep love for you motivate you to live out your love for Him back?

_____

_____

Don't let the enemies voice drown out the GREAT and precious promises spoken over you as a believer dear one!! Micah 7:8 (NIV) *Do not gloat over me, my enemy! Though I have fallen, I will rise. Though I sit in darkness, the LORD will be my light.* The Light in you can not be overcome by darkness, don't succumb to the darkness! *The light shines in the darkness, and the darkness has not overcome it.* John 1:5 (NIV) *For with you is the fountain of life; in your light we see light.* Psalm 36:9 (NIV)

Let's glance forward to the book of 1 Peter 5:2-4 and record how you see Jesus' love and Truth spoken over Peter's life taking root.

_____

_____

How do you see evidence that God's Truth is taking root in your life?

_____

_____

Maybe ask a close friend how they see His Truth taking root in your life and share with them how you see His Truth taking root in theirs.

Isaiah 61:3 tells me you were made to be a display of His splendor dear one!! *…They will be called oaks of righteousness, a planting of the LORD for the display of his splendor.* (NIV) When the Lord plants within you and you remain steadfast in His Truth you will grow! Wow right!!! Amazing grace lavished on all who would receive Him!

After the call back of Peter, Jesus doesn't sugar coat anything. Re-read John 15:18-21 and remember how He has told us following Him will not be easy (John 16:33) and if we think we can come up with a better way than Jesus Himself, to share the gospel without experiencing rejection we are headed for a rude awakening I'm afraid. God wants us to go in with eyes wide open. There is clearly a cost yet the reward will far outweigh any cost. 2 Corinthians 4:17 (NIV) states, *For our light and momentary troubles are achieving for us an eternal glory that far outweighs them all.*

What exactly is Paul calling light and momentary in that verse? For many troubles do not seem light and momentary! Check out 2 Corinthians 11:23-27. ___ This Scripture will shed some light on the subject for us.

Yikes! Yet Mark 8:36 (NLT) reminds us, ...*what do you benefit if you gain the whole world but lose your own soul?* It's easy to get strung up on comparing trial to trial or success to success or even failure to success between ourselves and others however what does Jesus say when Peter starts to wonder how his buddy John will fair?! See John 21:22-23.

...*what is that to you? You must follow me.* John 21:22 (NIV) Jesus instructs us to keep our eyes on Him not on those around us. Do not get distracted dear one, in Christ you have been given a GREAT commission! The Author of all time doesn't waste it. God does not give busy work! The effort to breath life into your lungs is not half baked and not to be taken for granted!

Let His unfailing love flow into your heart as you then feed His sheep from the overflow. When we turn from sin and face toward God, confessing our sin He says...

You are forgiven, set free... now come, follow Me. *for though the righteous fall seven times, they rise again,...* Proverbs 24:16 (NIV) You were made to be a vessel of His overcoming victory! Oh praise the victorious One!!

Please record what you would like to remember most from today's study.

_____

_____

_____

_____

Day 6 & 7: A Time To Reflect

Over the next two days take time to reflect over your week of study. Maybe you need some time to catch up on the study material and this might be the perfect break to do just that with the Lord!

I encourage you to glance back at the final point at the end of each day that you recorded having had the greatest impact on your heart. As you spend time with God in prayer, reflect and record on the lines below how God is tying it all together and applying it to your life.

Ask that God make it clear who He would have you invite into a natural opportunity to share Him, to apply what you are learning. Trust Him to continue to take the lead. May we have a heart ever ready with eyes and ears out to the opportunities God wants to invite us into for His glory and praise.

Do not merely listen to the word, and so deceive yourselves. Do what it says. Anyone who listens to the word but does not do what it says is like someone who looks at his face in a mirror and, after looking at himself, goes away and immediately forgets what he looks like. But whoever looks intently into the perfect law that gives freedom, and continues in it - not forgetting what they have heard, but doing it - they will be blessed in what they do. James 1:22-25 (NIV)

_____

_____

_____

_____

_____

Philippians 4:13 (NIV) *I can do all things through him who gives me strength.*

John 14:26 (NIV) *But the Advocate, the Holy Spirit, whom the Father will send in my name, will teach you all things and will remind you of everything I have said to you.*

WEEK 9

Jesus also did many other things. If they were all written down, I suppose the whole world could not contain the books that would be written. John 21:25 (NLT)

Day 1: To The End Of Time... And Beyond!

Hello my friend. Today we will finish our walk through the harmony of the four gospels!! My emotions are mixed as I feel the exhilaration of having reached the top of a mountain however the climb was so spectacular that I am sad to see it come to an end! Praise the Lord His Word is like a sweet onion with infinite layers! No matter how many times you read the same passage you can get something living and actively different as well as applicable to real life, every single time! I pray we continue our quest for more of Him with ever increasing cravings of insatiable hunger only quenched by ever increasing amounts of Him! Please bow with me before the mighty, matchless, victorious, King of kings and Lord of lords and thank Him for how far He has brought us as we ask His help in finishing strong, making growth in Him the fruit of our labor.

Please walk with me through His great commission in Matthew 28:16-20 _____ and Mark 16:15-18. _____

Here we see once again that God's mission is world wide, for ALL people to come to know Him. *For God so loved the world that he gave his one and only Son, that whoever believes in him shall not perish but have eternal life.* John 3:16 (NIV)

This commission contains the last words Jesus leaves us with so it must be of utmost importance. He issues a command not an option. The command is to go and do what according to Matthew 28:19-20?

Make disciples. Disciples are those that repent of sin, trust in Jesus as their Savior and try to live obedient to His commands.

Make disciples of all the nations. This was always God's plan. He has never left plan "A"... His plan from the fall in Genesis 3 has always been to bring all people back to Himself, to save those willing to receive the Savior, Jesus Christ. The enemy was always destined for defeat, ...*he will crush his head,...* Gen. 3:15 (NIV), and ALL those who would receive Jesus as their Savior would be blessed. Gen. 12:3 (NIV) ...*all peoples on earth will be blessed...* Gen. 18:18 (NIV) ...*all nations on earth will be blessed...*

Throughout all of time nothing and no one could thwart God Almighty's plan "A" for you and I!! How does this embolden your faith?

Matthew 28:19 refers to baptizing in the name of Who?

Father, Son and Holy Spirit yet the word name is not plural in that verse it is singular giving evidence to the Trinity. God, three in one.

Baptism is a public display of a persons choice to be identified as a believer in Jesus as their personal Savior and God. Jesus Himself gave us His example to follow while on this earth in every way; thought, word and action. He participated in baptism (Matthew 3:13-17). We are saved by faith in Jesus. Baptism is an act of obedience and symbolizes a willing submission of ones life to live not for themselves but for God. In a sense, the old nature is dying and being washed away through immersion and the new cleansed life of the believer begins in the rising up out of the water.

2 Corinthians 5:17 (NIV) *Therefore, if anyone is in Christ, the new creation has come: The old has gone, the new is here!*

We are commissioned with the command to tell others the Truth we know. Maybe that means go overseas and maybe that means we are to cross the pool deck and share the Truth with our neighbor. God knows the details of your individual plan, He knows your steps in His GREAT commission. So, *Trust in the LORD with all your heart and lean not on your own understanding; in all your ways submit to him, and he will make your paths straight.* Proverbs 3:5-6 (NIV)

Jesus did come as King of the world, not as a military leader but rather a King who can overcome strongholds and reigns in faithfulness and victorious Truth within every human heart that will accept Jesus Christ as Lord and Savior; the Way, the Truth, and the Life (John 14:6)!

Please walk with me further through Mark 16:19-20 _____ and Luke 24:50-53 _____ as we see Jesus ascend into heaven.

Where does Jesus take a seat according to Mark 16:19?

_____

At the right hand of God. Signifying His victory, His completion of the work started before time as we know it! *...the Lamb who was slain from the creation of the world.* Revelation 13:8 (NIV) *...Look, the Lion of the tribe of Judah, the heir to David's throne, has won the victory....* Revelations 5:5 (NLT)

This same victorious God who has not faltered from plan "A" throughout all of time and proves faithful to finish that which He starts will do the same with your life dear one. *being confident of this, that he who began a good work in you will carry it on to competition until the day of Christ Jesus.* Philippians 1:6 (NIV) *And we know that in all things God works for the good of those who love him, who have been called according to his purpose.* Romans 8:28 (NIV)

What emotion is depicted in Luke 24:52?

_____

Great joy! During an event that most surely blew their ever lovin' minds they were moved with great joy! Through what? WORSHIP! Worshiping even when our mood doesn't match our mission is when we begin to truly trust Him in all that we do not see and have yet to understand. That is where we will find great joy. A joy that runs deeper than happiness, which shifts with a mood dictated by outward events. In Jesus there is a joy that remains steadfast and true because we are held firm and secure by the Faithful and True who has overcome this world.

Please continue with me to our last few verses today found in John 20:30-31_____ and John 21:24-25. _____

Both of these segments of Scripture in John 20 and 21 tell us there are a great many things not recorded, if they were, probably the whole world could not even contain the amount of books it would take!!! Wow!! Can you not wait to dive into the archives held in heaven with me!!!?!!! But the fact remains the things that were recorded are everything we need to know to believe here on earth.

Often we want to know certain details within specific situations in our lives but we can trust that the God who does know and holds all the details in His mighty capable hands, will make known to us all the details that are pertinent to our ability of walking faithfully with Him.

We are on a need to know basis and often we don't need to know (as much as we may think we need to)! We know the One who does know, we can remember His heart toward us, how He has always proven faithful in the past and rest in that which we do know, to embolden our faith in all that we don't. Always go back to what you know… go back to the Scriptures you have studied here, look back over your rocks of remembrance, your stones of Truth within the Scriptures you have studied that have built up an unshakable foundation within your heart and mind… *so that you may continue to believe that Jesus is the Messiah, the Son of God, and that by believing in him you will have life by the power of his name.* John 20:31 (NLT)

Trust Him who is faithful and who's promises are true. Remember no matter what, Jesus loves you.

And remember Jesus says, …*surely I am always with you always, to the very end of the age."* Matthew 28:20 (NIV)

Please take a moment to record what you would like to remember most from today's study.

_____
_____
_____
_____

Day 2: Wait…When?!

Hello my friend. The rest of this week through next will look a bit different in that we will not be in the gospels as much, but rather we will be moving through a few other books of the Bible. We will take some time to look at examples of those who struggled with the unknown like we often do and yet chose to be a vessel of His victory, a reflection of His greater story. The hope is that their stories of faith might embolden ours so that we too might become a brighter reflection of His victory, fanning the flame of faith for future generations to come!

We will study how these biblical characters were able to overcome through a shift of focus from what they didn't know to Who they did know. We will study a character who also struggled with where she belonged amidst the tragic events of her life and yet found her victory wrapped up in the Victorious One.

We will study the important command to make known His faithfulness to the generations and we will gaze at characters whose lives proclaimed the remembrance of His faithfulness, boldly embarking into their future fully trusting that the God who had thus far helped them, could be trusted to help them again.

Praying as we embark further on these final two weeks that He conforms us more into the image of His Son; Who while here on earth painted the best picture for us of how to effectively serve selflessly, love faithfully and trust unwaveringly in our Heavenly Father.

Let's begin shall we!

After leading off in prayer that He lead us into deeper revelations of Himself and that our hearts are prepared to receive that which He brings us, please meet me on the other side of Acts chapter 1:1-11. _____

Acts 1 opens like a sequel to the gospel Luke as it is Luke writing the book of Acts as well! Who does Luke address in Luke 1:3?

_____

Who does Luke address once more in Acts 1:1?

___

Theophilus. This name means, "loved by God" or "one who loves God". As one who loves God, and whom God loves, doesn't knowing this make the book feel a bit more personal being addressed in this manner?!

In Acts 1:3 how many days does it record Jesus remained on earth appearing from time to time to the apostles between His resurrection and ascension?

___

Forty.

According to Acts 1:3 what did He continue to prove and what did He speak about?

___

Proving He was actually alive and He spoke about the Kingdom of God.

What is the promised gift Jesus instructs His disciples to wait for in Acts 1:4-5?

___

The gift of the Holy Spirit.

How do the following Scriptures depict the gift of the Holy Spirit to us?

Romans 15:13 (NIV) *May the god of hope fill you with all joy and peace as you trust in him, so that you may overflow with hope by the power of the Holy Spirit.*

2 Corinthians 3:17 (NIV) *Now the Lord is the Spirit, and where the Spirit of the Lord is, there is freedom.*

1 Corinthians 6:19-20 (NIV) *Do you not know that your bodies are temples of the Holy Spirit, who is in you, whom you have received from God? You are not your own; you were bought at a price. Therefore honor God with your bodies.*

John 14:26 (NIV) *But the Advocate, the Holy Spirit, whom the Father will send in my name, will teach you all things and will remind you of everything I have said to you.*

Romans 5:5 (NIV) *And hope does not put us to shame, because God's love had been poured out into our hearts through the Holy Spirit, who has been given to us.*

1 Corinthians 2:11 (NIV) *For who knows a person's thoughts except their own spirit within them? In the same way no one knows the thoughts of God except the Spirit of God.*

Mark 13:11 (NIV) *Whenever you are arrested and brought to trial, do not worry beforehand about what to say. Just say whatever is given you at the time, for it is not you speaking, but the Holy Spirit.*

John 15:26 (NIV) *"When the Advocate comes, whom I will send to you from the Father —the Spirit of truth who goes out from the Father—he will testify about me.*

Romans 8:26 (NIV) *In the same way, the Spirit helps us in our weakness. We do not know what we ought to pray for, but the Spirit himself intercedes for us through wordless groans.*

Briefly describe in your own words who the Spirit is and what the Spirit does according to these verses.

_____

_____

How willing are we to wait for this kind of help, this kind of power in our daily moments within our thoughts, words and actions?

_____

_____

1 Thessalonians 5:19 (NIV) states, *Do not quench the Spirit.* That means that in God's amazing grace He has given us free will to choose our own way; coupled with the words of wisdom that quenching the helping hand He extends will not end well for us. *For the foolishness of God is wiser than human wisdom, and the weakness of God is stronger than human strength.* 1 Corinthians 1:25 (NIV)

Read the benefits of waiting on the Lord according to the following verses.

Lamentations 3:25 (ESV) *The Lord is good to those who wait for him, to the soul who seeks him.*

Psalm 40:1 (NIV) *I waited patiently for the Lord; he turned to me and heard my cry.*

Isaiah 40:31 (NKJV) *But those who wait on the LORD Shall renew their strength; They shall mount up with wings like eagles, They shall run and not be weary, They shall walk and not faint.*

Isaiah 30:18 (NIV) *Yet the LORD longs to be gracious to you; therefore he will rise up to show you compassion. For the LORD is a God of justice. Blessed are all who wait for him!*

Psalm 5:3 (NIV) *In the morning, Lord, you hear my voice; in the morning I lay my requests before you and wait expectantly.*

James 5:8 (NIV) *You too, be patient and stand firm, because the Lord's coming is near.*

Psalm 37:9 (NKJV) *For evildoers shall be cut off; But those who wait on the Lord, They shall inherit the earth.*

Hebrews 10:36 (NLT) *Patient endurance is what you need now, so that you will continue to do God's will. Then you will receive all that he has promised.*

Jude 1:21 (NIV) *keep yourselves in God's love as you wait for the mercy of our Lord Jesus Christ to bring you to eternal life.*

Record in your own words some of the benefits of waiting on the Lord according to these verses.

_____

_____

In Acts 1:6 what did the disciples keep on asking Jesus?

_____

When?!?!? When will you bring Your Kingdom?

How often do we want to know the schedule?! When, Lord, please just tell me when!!!

How does Jesus respond to their, "When?!" in Acts 1:7-8?

_____

He does not give them "when", He gives them the promise of Himself and the power of His Spirit. Just as He gives us!! The rest was/is *"...not for you to know."* (NLT) If God has not revealed a certain detail to us it's because we don't need to know it yet. We can continue to pray our uncertainty over to Him and wait and watch and walk in step with Him; trusting that if the time comes that we need to know, He will not forget to make it clear, whatever "it" is by His Spirit within us.

However in Acts 1:8 He does give us what we should be doing while we are waiting on "when". What is it?

_____

Telling people about Him!

How are you telling people about Him right where you are at?

_____

From Acts 1:8 I also gather I don't always need to know everything, BUT I do know Who is with me and by what strength I will be able to accomplish His purpose through me. This same verse also gives me a way to "be". It says "be" His witness, not "do" His witness. If we just "be" in Him, He will work out the witness thing through our abiding in Him; just spend time with Him in prayer and in His Word.

Acts 1:11 issues another question that is almost comical. What question is stated in verse 11?

_____

Have you ever been standing around just staring into the clouds?! The angels saw the disciples starring up into the sky and they asked, why?! Yes, Jesus has been taken to heaven...BUT... it's not the end! Do you have a situation or circumstance that is leaving you perplexed? Does it help to know that in Jesus, whatever it is, it is not your end?!! The angels tell the perplexed disciples that one day God will return from heaven in the same way they saw Him go! (Acts 1:11 NLT) Dear one, He is coming back to take us to to be with Him in His Kingdom!! This is not our end!

We may not understand it all but we know He is with us and the power of The Spirit will enable us. We also know He is returning for us so meanwhile we can just BE in Him! As we abide in Him, He will produce fruit from our lives that witnesses to His Good News. (See John 14:1-6 and John 15:5.)

Let's glance at Numbers 9:15-23. _____

This is a wild portion of Scripture is it not!?!! It instructs me in the specific dance steps of the "depenDANCE"! It's only through dependence on Him that we will be able to dance through this life well.

Let's look specifically at one step in Numbers 9:22 (NIV) *Whether the cloud stayed over the tabernacle for two days or a month or a year, the Israelites would remain in camp and not set out; but when it lifted, they would set out.*

Anyone else start to twitch with that kind of schedule?! I mean isn't it lacking all the details I need to adequately prepare!!?! There is a big difference in what

I pack in my suitcase for two days as opposed to a year! However in the cloud of His faithful presence we find that the details of the schedule are not missing, just left in The Hands big enough to handle them. Sometimes it's only in the clouds that we begin to see most clearly what truly matters.

Thank you for your diligence in study today. Please recored the point that God impacted your heart with the most as you spent time in His Word.

_____

_____

_____

_____

Day 3: Feel The Heat!

Hello beloved of God. I'm glad you came, the party is gonna heat up today! Let's bow before our God who declares His Word to be like fire. Let's ask that He help us correctly handle His Word of Truth and that He reveal great and unsearchable things we do not know.

Let's savor the fire of Acts 2! _____

Can you just imagine!!?!! Just faithfully meeting together, trying to encourage one another and all of a sudden a "WHEN" arrives at the moment you least expected it! Because you were faithfully following through in obedience within the mundane, your ordinary became the grounds for something extraordinary!!

Describe the scene according to the details given in Acts 2:1-4.

_____

_____

The Holy Spirit filled that place, filled them and equipped them far beyond themselves!

I pray that out of his glorious riches he may strengthen you with power through his Spirit in your inner being, so that Christ may dwell in your hearts through faith. And I pray that you, being rooted and established in love, may have power, together with all the Lord's holy people, to grasp how wide and long and high and deep is the love of Christ, and to know this love that surpasses knowledge-- that you may be filled to the measure of all the fullness of God. Ephesians 3:16-19 (NIV)

Acts 2:12 paints the picture of everyone's confusion at the amazing things taking place! Filled with the power of the Spirit Peter steps forward (vs. 14).

And pray for me, too. Ask God to give me the right words so I can boldly explain God's mysterious plan that the Good News is for Jews and Gentiles alike. Ephesians 6:19 (NLT)

When they saw the courage of Peter and John and realized that they were unschooled, ordinary men, they were astonished and they took note that these men had been with Jesus. Acts 4:13 (NIV)

For God has not given us a spirit of fear, but of power and of love and of a sound mind. 2 Timothy 1:7 (NKJV)

We see Peter step forward in sheer God-confidence and clarify the people's questions with Scripture just as Jesus used Scripture to combat the enemy in the desert (Matthew 4:1-11)!

Hebrews 4:12 (NIV) *For the word of God is alive and active. Sharper than any double-edged sword, it penetrates even to dividing soul and spirit, joints and marrow; it judges the thoughts and attitudes of the heart.*

What does Hebrews 10:35-39 tell us about God-confidence?

_____

_____

Don't throw it away! You were not made to shrink back! You will be richly rewarded for your faithful endurance!

Wait for the Lord; be strong and take heart and wait for the Lord. Psalm 27:14 (NIV)

The Lord is not slow in keeping his promise, as some understand slowness. Instead he is patient with you, not wanting anyone to perish, but everyone to come to repentance. But the day of the Lord will come like a thief. The heavens will disappear with a roar; the elements will be destroyed by fire, and the earth and everything done in it will be laid bare. Since everything will be destroyed in this way, what kind of people ought you to be? You ought to live holy and godly lives as you look forward to the day of God and speed its coming. That day will bring about the destruction of the heavens by fire, and the elements will melt in the heat. But in keeping with his promise we are looking forward to a new heaven and a new earth, where righteousness dwells. 2 Peter 3:9-13 (NIV)

Wait ready for our God is coming back!! (As my son might exclaim it, "…and He's comin' in hot!!") Hallelujah and Amen!!!

Please record that which you would like to remember the most.

_____

_____

_____

_____

I saw heaven standing open and there before me was a white horse, whose rider is called Faithful and True. With justice he judges and wages war. His eyes are like blazing fire, and on his head are many crowns. He has a name written on him that no one knows but he himself. He is dressed in a robe dipped in blood, and his name is the Word of God. The armies of heaven were following him, riding on white horses and dressed in fine linen, white and clean. Coming out of his mouth is a sharp sword with which to strike down the nations. "He will rule them with an iron scepter." He treads the winepress of the fury of the wrath of God Almighty. On his robe and on his thigh he has this name written: king of kings and lord of lords. Revelation 19:11-16 (NIV)

Day 4: The Glow Of Living Hope

…Let the weakling say, "I am strong!" Joel 3:10 (NIV)

Hello friend! Today we begin our trek through the life of a most courageous gal named Ruth! She had lived and searched the land over and found none to compare to the victorious God of Israel! Her story as recorded in the four chapters within the book of the Bible titled "Ruth", is one of intense intrigue. Your heart is sure to be caught up in the drama and soar in the Truth as God reveals it. The Truth that no story is too far gone for our God to bring beautiful victory where once lay only bitter ash.

Please bow with me in prayer before we begin. Psalm 25:4-5 (NIV) *Show me your ways, Lord, teach me your paths. Guide me in your truth and teach me, for you are God my Savior, and my hope is in you all day long.*

If you remember back to our first week of study we touched on the genealogy of Jesus found in Matthew 1. We highlighted some of the kings listed, now please take another brief moment to glance over the first 17 verses of that chapter and record the only four ladies mentioned in Jesus genealogy (aside from His mother Mary).

Tamar - verse 3, Rahab - verse 5, Ruth - verse 5, Bathsheba - verse 6

Now if you have been traveling with us through the other books in this L.I.G.H.T. series you will have already had a chance to go deeper into the lives of Rahab, Bathsheba and Tamar. Now we will get to dive into the life of Ruth, another gal the world would have grafted out and yet Jesus saw fit to graft her straight into His very genealogy! He made us ALL to be vessels of His victory!

Oh please take a moment to savor the Truth of Romans 11:11-24 and praise the God who is able! _____

These four women may have come from shady pasts yet chose to step into the victorious Truth God held out to them. They became vessels of His victory when they chose to trust Him, to fix their eyes on Him rather than the world, their past, their situation, the other voices in their heads… They became vessels if His victory when they chose to rest their hearts and minds in His overcoming Truth. Now they could live set free, led forth, led out, in His triumphal procession… victorious! You can too dear one. You were made to be a vessel of His victory too!

But thanks be to God, who always leads us as captives in Christ's triumphal procession and uses us to spread the aroma of the knowledge of him everywhere. 2 Corinthians 2:14 (NIV) Please circle the world "always" in that verse. We are only ever led in overcoming triumph when we follow Jesus! Abide in Him always and always you will be in victory!

Now for the awaited book of Ruth! As we dive in let's keep in mind that the entire Old Testament is a foreshadowing of the coming Christ. It all points to Jesus. So in this book of Ruth, the character Ruth, (whose name means friendship) is actually a picture of us, the church or the Bride of Christ. Boaz, whose name means standing in strength, is a representation of Jesus our Redeemer.

Please read Ruth 1. ____

This story begins with an epically sad start! However we see Ruth place her hope in a faith that would prove trustworthy in the face of insurmountable odds and become her saving grace.

Where did this family start out living before they moved (Ruth 1:1)?

_____

Bethlehem in Judah. Bethlehem means house of bread and Judah means praise! We can choose to praise God because He remains to be the Bread of Life in all situations (John 6:35).

What made them leave Bethlehem?

_____

A famine. It would make logical sense to leave and go find another place but Isaiah 55:8-9 tells us He has ways beyond our tracing out so let's make sure we bring Him not only the things we don't think we understand in prayer but also those things that we think we do. We need to make sure it is God leading us out and not us running away.

Naomi's family leaves for Moab in search of a better life situation. Moab started in a cave (See. Gen 19 - Moab doesn't have a real heathy history.) In Psalm 108:9 God calls Moab His washbasin. Naomi's family left the house of bread for a washbasin! After 10 years there Naomi was ready to wash her hands of the heartbreaking memories that occurred in Moab. However God will redeem even the move to Moab. Ruth (who will become the great-grandmother of king David) comes out of Moab... who would have thought?! That has God's Ephesians 3:20 stamp all over it! If you have a "move to Moab" moment/season don't doubt that God can still use His Ephesians 3:20 stamp all over it too, dear one.

Ephesians 3:20 (NIV) *Now to Him who is able to do immeasurably more than all we ask or imagine, according to his power that is at work within us,*

Think back. Have you ever made a choice you thought made sense at the time only to find that maybe you should have brought that "good idea" before the Lord before you acted on it?

_____

Have you since seen evidence of God's grace and redemptive work through that possibly poor decision?

_____

If not yet, bring it to the Lord, Romans 8:28 tells us there is not one thing He can't work together for our good and His glory.

Elimelech's (Naomi's husband) name means God is my King. Yet he got off course it would seem and went to live in a pagan land where God was not held as King and it was his kids, the next generation that paid the price. What choices are you making today that prove you hold God as your King to the next generation?

_____

Naomi waited where she was until she heard that the Lord had blessed His people (Ruth 1:6). Isaiah 30:18 (NIV) ... *Blessed are all who wait for him!*

Hardships can sometimes be the best tuners for our ears to receive Truth. Naomi sure had experienced enough hardship and her ears were tuned to the blessing of the Lord.

What have you experienced that has brought your focus, your mind and heart, back to where it belongs?

_____

Naomi now is left in a desperate state mentally and physically. She is in a foreign land and her whole family, her husband and children have all died yet she is left with two (very different than her) daughters-in-law from this foreign, pagan land.

Can you imagine yourself in any one of these three ladies positions? How might you feel? List how you might respond or feel in each of the ladies shoes below.

Naomi:

_____

Orpah:

_____

Ruth:

_____

Is there one lady you can relate to more than another for any reason?

_____

No matter who you identify with more we have a God who identifies with us. Hebrews 4:15 (NIV) states, _For we do not have a high priest who is unable to empathize with our weaknesses,…_ He knows where we are weak dear one and it doesn't scare Him away!

Naomi feels bad and doesn't want her daughter's-in-law to be dragged into her situation any further. So she urges them to go back home (as she herself goes back to her own home) to find new husbands. According to Ruth 1:14 (below) what do each of the girls decide to do?

_____

_____

Verse 14 (NLT), *And again they wept together, and Orpah kissed her mother-in-law good-bye. But Ruth clung tightly to Naomi.*
Please circle the words "clung tightly to" in the above verse.

Check out Hebrews 10:23 and Joshua 23:8 (listed below) and record what those verses say we are to cling tightly to?

_____

_____

Hebrews 10:23 (NLT) *Let us hold tightly without wavering to the hope we affirm, for God can be trusted to keep his promise.*
Joshua 23:8 (NLT) *Rather, cling tightly to the LORD your God as you have done until now.*

We are to cling to our hope in Jesus! Ruth was from a pagan land and Naomi knew God Almighty. I wonder if what made Ruth cling to Naomi and refuse to leave her was that she saw a hope glowing from Naomi that she wanted! A Living Hope that glowed EVEN IF…, EVEN WHEN…, EVEN THOUGH…

Ruth went with Naomi while Naomi was in her trying times. If we too are willing to show the world God is still God and still victoriously good in our trials, they just might be more drawn to our Jesus.

What does Ruth say at the end of Ruth 1:16?

_____

Your God will be my God. Ruth was willing to give up everything she knew to cling tightly to the something different she saw in Naomi! Naomi, even in her sad situation had a glow of hope that drew in Ruth. As a believer in Jesus do you emulate that glow of hope that would draw others into the body of Christ? This is not a glow we can produce on our own. This glow is produced by His Spirit within us. That fire is stoked through time spent abiding in His presence via prayer and in His Word.

John 15:5 (NIV) *"I am the vine; you are the branches. If you remain in me and I in you, you will bear much fruit; apart from me you can do nothing.*

In Ruth 1:19-20 we see the whole town is stirred by Naomi's return. She must have been quite the influential individual! What characteristics in a person stir your heart with positive emotions?

_____

Were gentle and humble on your list too? I know those are characteristics of Jesus (Matthew 11:29) and the more time we spend with God the more we will begin to look like His Son.

The barley harvest was taking place at the time Ruth and Naomi went back to Naomi's home (Ruth 1:22). This was also Passover time. Passover is when the last supper eventually took place as Jesus became The Passover Lamb. You and I come to our eternal Home through the belief that Jesus is the Lamb of God. Through belief in Jesus' death and resurrection we have a a way to come into our Heavenly home! (John 14:6)

50 days following Passover comes Pentecost. That is when we will eventually see Boaz marry Ruth! Remember Boaz represents Jesus and Ruth the Bride of Christ! At Pentecost the Holy Spirit was poured out into the believers and

many more believed (Remember Acts 2!!!). When we enter into a relationship with Jesus He sends His Holy Spirit to fill and overflow us with hope from within!

Romans 15:13 (NIV) *May the God of hope fill you with all joy and peace as you trust in him, so that you may overflow with hope by the power of the Holy Spirit.*

Naomi has returned home however when the whole town is happy to see her what is her response? What is her specific request?

_____

Don't call me Naomi, (which means pleasant) but call me Mara, (which means bitter).

Lets take a bit of a rabbit trail down Exodus 15:22-27. ____ (This will be a worthwhile venture, I promise!)

What was the name of the place Moses came to and found the water was bitter?

_____

Marah. Similar in name and also means bitter! But Who made that situation go from bitter to sweet?

_____

The God who heals! It took a bitter situation for God to reveal more of who He was and wanted to be to them… He is the God who heals! Maybe the bitterness Naomi felt was God stretching her heart to receive a bigger blessing then she ever could have imagined.

So let's proceed deeper into this Ruth saga. Who does Naomi feel has brought this bitter situation upon her? (See Ruth 1:21)

_____

Almighty God. God only allows things to sift through His nail scared hands into our lives that He can use for our good and His glory. We must choose to trust beyond what our physical eyes can see and our physical ears can hear and what our finite mind can conceive.

1 Corinthians 2:9 (NIV) *However, as it is written: "What no eye has seen, what no ear has heard, and what no human mind has conceived"— the things God has prepared for those who love him—*

Let's look at Isaiah 53:11-12 (NLT) which depicts Jesus suffering on the cross. *When he sees all that is accomplished by his anguish, he will be satisfied. And because of his experience, my righteous servant will make it possible for many to be counted righteous, for he will bear all their sins. I will give him the honors of a victorious soldier, because he exposed himself to death. He was counted among the rebels. He bore the sins of many and interceded for rebels.*

Because of Jesus' death and resurrection we don't have to end in bitterness! He is able to use every drop of bitterness we feel and turn it for our good and His glory! If we choose to walk IN faith ON the promises of God UNTO death (because faith sees BEYOND death) we will end in sweet glory! Cling to the glow of LIVING HOPE!

Romans 8:28 (NIV) *And we know that in all things God works for the good of those who love him, who have been called according to his purpose.* 1 Peter 1:3 (NIV) *Praise be to the God and Father of our Lord Jesus Christ! In his great mercy he has given us new birth into a living hope through the resurrection of Jesus Christ from the dead,*

Please record the point of greatest impact to your heart today.

_____

_____

_____

_____

Day 5: Amazing Grace

Welcome back my friend! Are you ready to dive into chapter 2 of Ruth like I am?!! Today we will be introduced to Boaz and as mentioned earlier he is the Old Testament's foreshadowing of Jesus, our ultimate Redeemer in the New Testament. Let's each begin first in prayer asking that God Almighty help us obediently follow His lead.

Let's begin!! Please read Ruth 2. ____

We pick up with Naomi and Ruth back in Bethlehem and Ruth decides it's time to find work to help them survive. When other gals her age were married and raising families, Ruth was picking up leftover grain stalks by anyone kind enough to allow her to. However, we never see it recorded that she grumbled or complained over even one day of it.

What is our attitude like in situations that might not be so ideal? How might we be intentional at remembering that what we choose to look for we usually find? If we look for the negative we will be sure to find it but if we look for the positive in all things how might that allow more room for God to invade us with His perspective?

I like to think of a pineapple. What at first may appear brown, spiky and rough just might end up being the brightest, sweetest thing ever if I'd take the time to look deeper!

Ruth goes out and where does Ruth 2:3 indicate she just "happened" to find herself?

_____

Ruth just happened to find herself in the field of a relative! A relative of her father-in-law!!! Of all the dangers a young unmarried women could have fallen into in her situation, God Almighty made sure to direct her steps to safety!! Proverbs 16:9 (NIV) reminds us, *In their hearts humans plan their course, but the Lord establishes their steps.*

Can you think of a time that in hindsight you KNOW God guided your steps and protected you from harm?

_____

Ruth may have felt lost and alone but God never lost sight of her. Dear one no matter how you feel, He has never lost sight of you either. Job 23:9-10 (NIV) *When he is at work in the north, I do not see him; when he turns to the south, I catch no glimpse of him. But he knows the way that I take; when he has tested me, I will come forth as gold.*

Speaking of God never losing sight of you… who did we say Boaz was to represent? And who notices Ruth in his field now in our story?

_____

Boaz!

In Ruth 2:4 we see Boaz come into town and go to be with the harvesters. Boaz foreshadows Jesus and Jesus came to earth from heaven to be Immanuel, God with us.

In Ruth 2:9 what is Ruth instructed to do freely when she is thirsty?

_____

Isaiah 12:3 (NIV) *With joy you will draw water from the wells of salvation.*

In Ruth 2:10 we see that Ruth can not fathom such kind treatment, such grace, such favor. Deuteronomy 23:3 (NIV) states, *No Ammonite or Moabite or any of their descendants may enter the assembly of the Lord, not even in the tenth generation.* Ruth, from the pagan land of Moab was a Moabite. Nothing and no one is past the reach of our God's gracious hand and heart. *Surely the arm of the LORD is not too short to save, nor his ear too dull to hear.* Isaiah 59:1 (NIV)

The gap between ourselves and our God is a chasm too wide to even comprehend, a chasm only He could have crossed to save and redeem us, and He did!! To realize this Truth brings us to fall on our faces in Holy reverent fear. We then recognize that to give our lives back to Him as a living sacrifice, to use as a magnification of His redeeming grace is not a sacrifice but rather a sheer honor.

Boaz had not only noticed Ruth but Ruth 2:11 indicates he has heard about her too. In verse 12 who does Boaz indicate Ruth has come under the wings of refuge and reward?

The LORD, the God of Israel.

Psalm 57:1 (NLT) *Have mercy on me, O God, have mercy! I look to you for protection. I will hide beneath the shadow of your wings until the danger passes by.*
Psalm 91:1 (NIV) *Whoever dwells in the shelter of the Most High will rest in the shadow of the Almighty.*
Hebrews 11:6 (NIV) *And without faith it is impossible to please God, because anyone who comes to him must believe that the exists and that he rewards those who earnestly seek him.*

Those wings of protection, and the reward of Him is available to you and I too.

In Ruth 2:13, Ruth thanks Boaz for his display of kindness even though she is not one of his regular workers. Where she may have felt like an outsider Boaz brought her inside. Jesus died so that we could all be made insiders! *Let us then approach God's throne of grace with confidence, so that we may receive mercy and find grace to help us in our time of need.* Hebrews 4:16 (NIV)

Remember in the Jewish temple a veil prevented just anyone from going into the Holy of Holies (the place were the Ark of the Covenant and God's presence resided). However when Jesus died on the cross do you remember what happen to that veil? (Hint: Matthew 27:50-51)

_____

The veil was torn! In what direction?

_____

Top to bottom! It was God's doing! Nothing man could have done could have made the crossing into His presence for eternity possible, only Jesus could do that. Hebrews 10:20 (NLT) *By his death, Jesus opened a new and life-giving way through the curtain into the Most Holy place.*

By Ruth 2:14 it's meal time and Boaz gave to Ruth and what does that last sentence in this verse say?

_____

Ruth was able to eat all she wanted and still had some left over!

You can never out-give God! Malachi 3:10 (NIV) *Bring the whole tithe into the storehouse, that there may be food in my house. Test me in this," says the LORD Almighty, "and see if I will not throw open the floodgates of heaven and pour out so much blessing that there will not be room enough to store it.*

He gives knowing we can't repay, He gives above and beyond fully knowing we can't ever pay back! Do we give this way, with such sacrificial love? With such trust in our Source that we can freely give of our resources? How might we allow God to invade us with His kind of love to freely and cheerfully give away that which we could never possibly run out of in Him?

Please read and record what True love is and looks like in 1 Corinthians 13:4-8.

_____

_____

Are you a picture of this? Do you hang out with people that are a picture of this?

What is Ruth welcomed to partake in, in Ruth 2:14?

_____

What a picture of communion! The end of verse 14 states that she ate until she had enough yet there was still some left over! In Jesus there is always more than enough. He is always going above and beyond our expectations and blowing our imaginations out of the water (Eph. 3:20) We can never out give or out sin the redeeming blood of Jesus (Romans 5:20). On the cross He said, "It is finished." (John 19:30) nothing more can be added. Jesus paid it all, ALL. Past, present and future. Life eternal cannot be bought, deserved or earned in any way. We enter through belief by faith.

Just as Boaz beckoned Ruth, "Come…" Revelation 22:17 is an invitation from our God extended to us all! (NIV) *The Spirit and the bride say, "Come!" And let the one who hears say, "Come!" Let the one who is thirsty come; and let the one who wishes take the free gift of the water of life.*

Do you think the workers in Ruth 2:16 had a right to protest and complain about what Boaz was asking them to do? Do you think the others may have thought it "unfair"?

Grace is never "fair" is it, and aren't we glad it's not!!!

Who might we be able to magnify His grace to by giving it away freely even though from the world's view it wouldn't be "fair"?

Who in our life would it be an honor to show grace to for Jesus sake?

Jesus redeemed our lives with such amazing grace even when it wasn't "fair". Jesus showed amazing grace taking our cross upon His shoulders to the death.

In Ruth 2:19 Naomi asks Ruth a question. What is it?

_____

"Where did you gather…?" Where do you gather? Where do you fill up? Is it at the feet of Jesus or somewhere else that can only offer less than?

Ruth just "happens" to wander into Boaz's field in 2:3 but it's not until 2:20 that Ruth is able to realize what this means! Have you ever experienced a gap between a blessing and realizing it was a blessing?

_____

Boaz means "standing in strength" Solomon named one of the two main temple pillars after his great-great grandfather Boaz (1 Kings 7:21)!! Ruth 2:20 (NIV) refers to Boaz as the guardian-redeemer. I don't know about you but it just makes Revelation 3:11-12 come to life for me!!! (See top of week 6.)

Isaiah 30:21 (NIV) reminds us, *Whether you turn to the right or tot he left your ears will hear a voice behind you, saying, "This is the way; walk in it."* How tuned into that voice are we? Do we trust Him to lead us or do we rush ahead and try to accomplish things our way when we can't quite see or understand God's way?

Remember Isaiah 30:18 tells us, *Yet the LORD longs to be gracious to you; therefore he will rise up to show you compassion. For the LORD is a God of justice. Blessed are all who wait for him!* So no one that waits on the Lord ends up missing out, rather they are blessed! May God help us (or at least me) be a better "waiter".

In Ruth 2:21, Ruth is excited to relay what she never could have imagined! Boaz had invited her to continue harvesting in his field through the season! Naomi is ecstatic with the news knowing Ruth will be safe with Boaz.

2 Thessalonians 3:3 also offers us a promise if we too will remain with God, our Standing Strength, our Redeemer. (NIV) *But the Lord is faithful, and he will strengthen you and protect you from the evil one.*

The Truth treasure found in 1 Corinthians 15:55-57 ____ explains why this is possible! Take a moment and read that passage then praise the victorious name of Jesus with me!

Ruth 2:23 indicates Ruth fell in right alongside the other women in the field. How well are we doing at getting along with the others God has placed alongside us on the playing field of life?

This saga is a page turner but let's stop here and let the Truth treasures God has uncovered for us take root in our hearts. By His amazing grace may He grow us up to live changed by them, becoming a brighter reflection of His Son to His glory and praise!

Please record what impacted your heart the most from your study today in His Word.

_____

_____

_____

_____

Day 6 & 7: A Time To Reflect

Over the next two days take time to reflect over your week of study. Maybe you need some time to catch up on the study material and this might be the perfect break to do just that with the Lord!

I encourage you to glance back at the final point at the end of each day that you recorded having had the greatest impact on your heart. As you spend time with God in prayer, reflect and record on the lines below how God is tying it all together and applying it to your life.

Ask that God make it clear who He would have you invite into a natural opportunity to share Him, to apply what you are learning. Trust Him to continue to take the lead. May we have a heart ever ready with eyes and ears out to the opportunities God wants to invite us into for His glory and praise.

Do not merely listen to the word, and so deceive yourselves. Do what it says. Anyone who listens to the word but does not do what it says is like someone who looks at his face in a mirror and, after looking at himself, goes away and immediately forgets what he looks like. But whoever looks intently into the perfect law that gives freedom, and continues in it - not forgetting what they have heard, but doing it - they will be blessed in what they do. James 1:22-25 (NIV)

_____

_____

_____

_____

_____

Philippians 4:13 (NIV) *I can do all things through him who gives me strength.*

John 14:26 (NIV) *But the Advocate, the Holy Spirit, whom the Father will send in my name, will teach you all things and will remind you of everything I have said to you.*

WEEK 10

Then Samuel took a stone and set it up between Mizpah and Shen. He named it Ebenezer, saying, "Thus far the LORD has helped us." 1 Samuel 7:12 (NIV)

Day 1: A Love Freely Given

Hi friend! Today Naomi begins the first "on-line dating" system… On line with God's ordained hook-up plan!! I tell you what there is nothing like His Living Word right! No "Bachelorette" show could hold a candle to this intrigue! Let's begin in prayer and then dive right in! *But the Advocate, the Holy Spirit, whom the Father will send in my name, will teach you all things and will remind you of everything I have said to you.* John 14:26 (NIV)

Please read Ruth 3. ____

In verse 3 what is the first thing Naomi tells Ruth to do?

_____

Wash herself or take a bath. Sticking with the symbolism that Boaz is a picture of Jesus and Ruth a picture of us, the bride of Christ, we too are to wash in the Word (Ephesians 5:26) and be ready for His second coming!

Remember what Matthew 24:36 tells us about the return of Jesus… (NIV) *"But about that day or hour no one knows, not even the angels in heaven, nor the Son, but only the Father.*
Keeping washed in the Word and living like you are ready for Jesus to return at any moment would surely be a way that would magnify His importance in your life to a watching world.

Are there some things you might intentionally change throughout the path of your day if you knew Jesus was going to return today?

In Ruth 3:4 (NIV) Naomi states, *He will tell you what to do."* Remember Boaz is a picture of Jesus and there is no one you would rather be taking advise from than the living Word Himself (John 1:1)!!!

John 14:26, the verse we prayed in our hearts as we started today tells us we have a helper, the Holy Spirit within us as believers, to help guide us. Record what 1 Kings 19:12-13 tells us about where God was found.

_____

God was in the whisper. Why does God whisper? Probably so we will lean in to His nearness!

John 10:27-28 holds such a hope filled promise! Lets tuck it into our hearts pocket shall we!? (NIV) *My sheep listen to my voice; I know them, and they follow me. I give them eternal life, and they shall never perish; no one will snatch them out of my hand.*

Ruth responds in obedience in Ruth 3:5. What does John 13:17 tell us?

_____

Memorizing the Word or just merely knowing it is not enough, we must DO what it says in obedience to receive the blessing from it. What if I only remembered in my head that walking into the street without looking for cars was a good idea but never did it?! I wouldn't last long!

Ruth chose to be obedient even when she may not have completely understood why or may have been completely unsure of the outcome. She was obedient even when she may have been tempted to completely rebel because life had not gone at all like she had probably planned. Do we choose to trust God like Ruth? We have all the unshakable promises of God written out for us now unlike Ruth did at that time. Will we take time in the gift of His Word and pray for ever increasing trust to remain faithfully obedient even when it's hard?!

In Ruth 3:6 we read that Ruth has gone to the threshing floor, willing to give of herself. Before that though, she had experienced Boaz making a sacrifice for her (a Moabite) in his field so that she could be filled, provided for and kept safe. When we begin to understand the incredible sacrifice of our God, how He laid down His life for ours, it stirs a willingness to give back of ourselves. It becomes an honor to give back even though nothing could ever repay Him for so great a sacrifice.

Recall Matthew 10:39 and what it has to say about when we choose to give our all to the One who gave us His all?

_____

What does Ruth ask Boaz to do for her in verse 9?

_____

Do we ever wonder in our heart of hearts if His blood could cover even that...even me...?! Oh yes dear one, those bones were never broken, remember! The very place blood is produced was never broken! (John 19:36)

Please fill in the blanks to Luke 11:10 (NIV) *For* _____ *who asks* _____; *the one who* _____ _____; *and to the one who* _____, *the door will be* _____. (Everyone, receives, seeks finds, knocks, opened)

Okay, did you too catch the joy in Boaz's words in the very next verse (Ruth 3:10)!!?! Oh the joy when love is given freely! To know you are loved truly, madly, deeply reminds me of Zephaniah 3:17 (NIV) *The LORD your God is with you, the Mighty Warrior who saves. He will take great delight in you; in his love he will no longer rebuke you, but will rejoice over you with singing."* God gives us free will and when we choose to love Him back... oh what joy! Luke 15:7 tells us there will be more joy in heaven over one sinner that repents than over ninety-nine righteous persons who do not need to repent. The Creator of all the earth rejoices over the gift of your love given back to Him freely!! Amazing!

In Ruth 3:10 what is Boaz taken with or find so becoming about Ruth's character?

_____

What does Matthew 6:19-21 relay to us about the kind of treasure we should value?

_____

Looking back at verse 10 in Ruth 3 we see how Ruth lived out this Truth in Matthew. How do you recognize ways in your own life that you live the Truth of Matthew 6:19-21 out?

_____

_____

Ruth 3:11 begins with what statement from Boaz (who we remember is a foreshadowing of Jesus)?

_____

Now don't worry about a thing, my daughter. ... (NLT)

Jesus tells us the very same thing directly in Luke 12:22-34. Please visit that address and record what stands out to you the most about that passage?

_____

_____

_____

_____

Worry and anxieties can sweep us off our feet unless we fix our eyes on Jesus the author and perfecter of our faith (Hebrews 12:2). We have this hope as an anchor for the soul, firm and secure (Hebrews 6:19). We can choose to worry which is futile. It gives us something to do but we get nowhere! Or we can choose to turn those thoughts into prayers and lay it all down a the Father's feet (1 Peter 5:7). The trick is not picking them up again once you have said "amen!".

We can develop a strategy for taking the offensive, rather than the defensive approach for when we feel a tidal wave of doubt or fear coming on. I like to keep a jar or note cards full of Scriptures by my bedside, even a list of the names of God. Reminding myself of Truth helps dispel the lies that threaten to overturn the ship at times. Float your mind on Who you have placed your faith in rather than let it flounder in overwhelming circumstances.

God is always bigger than our situation and the sun will always rise tomorrow (unless Jesus decides to return before hand), my dad says. Somehow this always helps me put things in perspective. *For as high as the heavens are above the earth, so great is his love for those who fear him;* Psalm 103:11 (NIV)

In Ruth 3:13 Boaz makes a bold statement when he says, I will redeem you myself! But isn't that a picture of what Jesus did for us! He redeemed us Himself because there was no way we could have done anything to accomplish the work.

By Ruth 3:16 Ruth is running home to share with Naomi EVERYTHING Boaz had done for her. Is this getting romantic or what! Can you just picture the giddy excitement these two women are sharing right now?!! Have we kept that giddy excited glow over our own romance with the King of kings and Lord of lords, so much so that we cannot keep from sharing the Good News with others either?!

Lets pray for a heightened awareness of the opportunities God presents to us on a daily basis so that we can share the Good News of what God has done for us. Don't worry about having the right words. If we need words Luke 12:12 reminds us, the Holy Spirit will teach us at the right time just what we should say. Maybe it will be by way of words or maybe it will be by way of action. We can pray not only to recognize the opportunities He presents but also for wisdom to know how to most effectively enter those opportunities. James 1:5 (NIV) reminds us, *If any of you lacks wisdom, you should ask God, who gives generously to all without finding fault, and it will be given to you.* Praise Him for that!

What is Naomi's advice to Ruth in Ruth 3:18?

_____

I see, that Ruth is told to be patient because Boaz won't rest until things are accomplished. Psalm 121:4 (NIV) reminds us, *indeed, he who watches over Israel will neither slumber nor sleep.* The One who watches over you does not sleep. (So we can!!!)

Lets rest here for now. Please record what has impacted your heart as you have studied in His Word today.

_____

_____

_____

_____

Day 2: Redeemed!

Hello dear friend. It is bitter sweet to come to this final chapter in Ruth, is it not?! I don't know that I'm ready for it to end… actually I'm not ready for this week to end as it is our final week of study together in this book! I do pray that as we close this chapter of our lives it will really just be the beginning of a deeper more grand adventure with our God as we embark onto the next page of our lives with His victory held steadfastly within!

Please bow with me to God's leadership in prayer, asking for willing hearts to receive His message in humble obedience.

Please savor Ruth chapter 4. ____

Remember back in Ruth chapter 3, specifically in Ruth 3:12, we learned that Boaz was not the closest redeemer, there was another and that my friends, is symbolic of the law. But now in chapter 4 verse 6 we see it stated that this one closer than Boaz, (the law) is unable to redeem! The law can not redeem us! That is why we need Jesus, God's amazing grace!!! Ruth 4:6 (NLT) states it this way, …*You redeem the land; I cannot do it."*

Romans 8:3 (NIV) *For what the law was powerless to do because it was weakened by the flesh, God did by sending his own son in the likeness of sinful flesh to be a sin offering. And so he condemned sin in the flesh,*

Now in Ruth 4:9-10 we read that Boaz indeed redeems Ruth! Please insert your name in the following verse.

But now, thus says the LORD, who created you, _____, *And He who formed you,* _____: *"Fear not, for I have redeemed you; I have called you by name; You are Mine. Isaiah 43:1 (NKJV)* *The blanks originally contain O Jacob and O Israel.

Ruth 4:11-12 seem to me like a blessing.

""The LORD bless you and keep you; the LORD make his face shine on you and be gracious to you; the LORD turn his face toward you and give you peace."' Numbers 6:24-26 (NIV)

Ruth 4:13 (NLT) states, *So Boaz took Ruth into his home…* Please record what John 14:3 tell us.

_____

In Ruth 4:13 we see Ruth, the Moabite, grafted in by faith to the very lineage of Jesus! But wait, back up to verse 12!! Please fill in the blanks below.
And may the LORD give you descendants by this young woman who will be like those of our ancestor Perez, the son of _____ *and*
_____. *(NLT)* (Tamar, Judah)

Tamar! The very same Tamar we spoke of earlier on day four of last week! She too was a foreigner like Ruth and yet was also included in the genealogy of Jesus in Matthew 1! It seems Jesus truly is a gift of great joy for ALL people willing to receive Him! John 10:16 and John 3:16 make it clear Jesus came to accomplish a world wide mission! John 10:16 (NIV) *I have other sheep that are not of this sheep pen. I must bring them also. They too will listen to my voice, and there shall be one flock and one shepherd.* John 3:16 (NIV) *For God so loved the world that he have his one and only Son, that whoever believes in him shall not perish but have eternal life.*

What are we doing to magnify His mission minded heart to the world?! He is a gift for ALL! He is a gift for YOU! Do not think you are outside the blessing.

Jesus said, "it is finished." on the cross, so don't continue to try and take up your shame and regret that He carried for you and cost Him His life! He rose victorious so that you could truly live set free from it all, not just part way, ALL the way!!

Naomi can be considered the prodigal daughter of Old Testament. She came back to Bethlehem where God renewed her just like His heart longs to do for us if we will come to Him, the Bread of Life.

Then all the women in the town said to Naomi... PRAISE THE LORD (verse 14)!!

Psalm 40:3 (NIV) *He put a new song in my mouth, a hymn of praise to our God. Many will see and fear the LORD and put their trust in him.*

In closing please fill in the blank according to Ruth 4:17 (NLT). *"Now at last _____ has a son again!"* (Naomi)

So that didn't say Mara?!?? NO! Jehovah-Rapha had redeemed the entire situation like only a Healing Redeemer could!

Joel 2:25 tells us He will repay you for the years the locusts have eaten! He is able to fully heal and redeem that which you thought was lost, that which was entirely bitter, He can make sweet again. He can give you a new name, a fresh start, a do over.

What seems too big to believe Him for today? Naomi thought she had lost it all, she assumed she would just go through life as a Mara but God redeemed her and said, no, what you thought would end in bitterness I will turn to sweetness beyond your wildest dreams!

Don't be so quick to put a period where God may have just placed a semicolon. Just wait and see, our perspective from eternity is coming. For now allow Him time to invade you with His life redeeming, life healing Truths. Hope in Him doesn't disappoint dear one.

The events in Ruth were part of God's plans and preparations for His coming Son, Jesus. Ruth was unaware of the greater purpose God was working out with her story. God used her faithful obedience in significant ways that even she would not see come to pass this side of heaven.

Jesus has promised His return (Rev. 19:11-16) and just as closely as God watched over every detail leading up to the birth of His Son, do you not think He is doing the very same thing over every detail leading up to His second coming!?!!

The significance of your life and mine will leave a legacy far beyond what we will be able to see this side of heaven. Let your legacy be one of faithful obedience like Ruth. When our past threatens to debilitate our effectiveness for His Kingdom, remember the cross, the thick flow of His never ending blood, His amazing redeeming grace and let His love just wash over you, revealing that where once may have only been handfuls of ash, now rises something breathtakingly beautiful! The old has gone the new has come (2 Cor. 5:17)! Live set free!!

Thank you, thank you, thank you for enduring with me till the end of this epic story - HIStory! Now go truly live yours, in magnification of His victory!

God bless you MUCHLY for finishing strong today. May He bless your faithful time spent in His living Word.

Please record that point that made the greatest impact on your heart today.

_____

_____

_____

_____

Day 3: Faithful Yesterday, Today and Forever

Hello and welcome! Thank you for coming and meeting with me today and in all the yesterdays too. After concluding (in day two this week) the epic love story recorded in Ruth, I hope you feel the Truth of His unfailing love falling a fresh on you today. By God's grace may we become ever stronger and more deeply rooted in Him through continued diligence in pursuing His heart back, forever in all our moments. As our moments (God willing) turn to hours, turn to days, turn to weeks, months and even years, we never want to forget all that we have learned over the past, near 10 weeks, and the implication it all holds on our lives.

Today, as we prepare to close out our time at the culmination of this week, we will study a Biblical example of one who made a diligent effort to not forget all that God had done. Might we learn from this record of events so that we too, will not forget the faithfulness of our victorious God.

Let's begin in prayer. May we be drawn in ever more closely to our Father's heart as His name is lifted high in honor.

Today our focus passage will mainly be 1 Samuel 7. _____ However if you would like to fill in more of the back story please take a few minutes and read through the intriguing saga beginning with 1 Samuel chapters 1-7! (I've also included a brief summary of these chapters on the next page or so.)

A brief back story summary of 1 Samuel 1-7:

◆ Samuel was a miraculous gift to Hannah, an answer to prayer after much hardship and barrenness. (1 Sam. 1:12-20)

◆ Hannah followed through with her promise to God and dedicated Samuel fully to the service of the Lord allowing Him to be raised in the Temple, rather than at their home in Ramah. (1 Sam. 1:24-28)

◆ 1 Sam. 2:18 (NLT) *But Samuel, though he was only a boy, served the LORD. He wore a linen garment like that of a priest.* 1 Sam. 2:21 (NLT) *...Samuel grew up in the presence of the Lord.*

◆ 1 Sam. 2:26 (NIV) *And the boy Samuel continued to grow in stature and in favor with the LORD and with people.*

◆ Eli, Israel's judge and high priest at the time had two sons that did evil. (1 Sam. 2:12-17)

- 1 Samuel 3 depicts young Samuels call to service. It took God calling little Sam four times before he recognized God's voice and responded to Him. 1 Samuel 3:10 (NLT) *And the LORD came and called as before, "Samuel! Samuel!" And Samuel replied, "Speak, your servant is listening."* It takes time in a relationship to learn the sound of someone's voice. God will not give up pursuing you; keep on pursuing Him in response. Romans 11:29 (NIV) *for God's gifts and his call are irrevocable.* Jeremiah 29:11-13 (NIV) *For I know the plans I have for you," declares the LORD, "plans to prosper you and not to harm you, plans to give you a hope and a future. Then you will call on me and come and pray to me, and I will listen to you. You will seek me and find me when you seek me with all your heart.*

- Due to the wickedness of Eli's sons and several generations of unfaithfulness God was bringing judgment and we see 1 Sam. 4 begin with devastating defeat in battle. 4,000 Israelites were left for dead. They thought maybe if they brought the Ark of the Covenant into battle they would be successful. However the second battle was far worse than the first losing a total of 30,000 Israelite lives including Eli and his two sons; AND the Ark was captured by the Philistine enemy!

- 1 Samuel 5 reveals the destruction of the enemy housing the captured Ark to the point they pass it off to other towns. However the same destruction continued to pursue the enemy that held the Ark.

- Finally in 1 Samuel 6 the enemy plots to return the Ark to Israel by tying two new mama cows (never tied to a cart before), to a cart and away from their babies! This cart was carrying the Ark and the golden guilt offerings from the five enemy towns that had been affected with destruction. Against all odds the mama cows separated themselves from their young and instinctively brought the Ark back to Israelite territory by cart!! 1 Samuel 6:18 (NLT) ...*The large rock at Beth-shemesh, where they set the Ark of the LORD, still stands in the field of Joshua as a witness to what happened there. A rock memorial to remember the faithfulness of our God!* Joel 2:25 (NIV) *"I will repay you for the years the locusts have eaten—...*

Hold up a moment, what kind of memorial did they set up to remember the faithfulness of God? (See above 1 Samuel 6:18.)

A ROCK memorial. Just tuck that tid bit of information in your pocket for later.

- ◆   The Ark was held in the home of Abinadab and his son Eleazar was ordained to be in charge of it. Here it remained for 20 years. (1 Sam. 7:1-2)

This is where we pick up our study today in 1 Samuel 7.

During the 20 years the Ark was with Eleazar the people mourned as they felt the Lord had abandoned them. What does Samuel urge the people to do in 1 Samuel 7:3?

He tells the people IF they are serious… GET RID of all their foreign gods and DETERMINE to OBEY ONLY the Lord. (Emphasis mine)

IF we are serious in growing in the Lord we must GET RID of all false gods in our life and DETERMINE to OBEY ONLY our Lord too! Our false god's might not be as obvious as a statue but what about a friendship, child, spouse, job?! Could any of these GOOD things take the place of your worship (subconsciously even) of the GREATEST One in your life? Whatever may hold position above God in our lives is something we need to ask God to dethrone. Then ask that He take His rightful place in our hearts and minds.

Addictions are also misplaced worship; strongholds that have hooked you into believing they will fill the void in your heart. Only God Almighty who knit your heart together knows how to adequately fill all the parts of your heart dear one.

For you created my inmost being; you knit me together in my mother's womb. I praise you because I am fearfully and wonderfully made; your works are wonderful, I know that full well. Psalm 139:13-14 (NIV)

The Lord is my light and my salvation - whom shall I fear? The Lord is the stronghold of my life - of whom shall I be afraid? Psalm 27:1 (NIV)

The Israelites responded positively to Samuel's urging in 1 Sam. 7:3, so in 1 Samuel 7:5 what does Samuel do for the people?

_____

What was poured out in verse 6?

_____

Water. A symbol of pouring out their hearts.

What did Samuel's mother say back in 1 Samuel 1:15?

_____

She was pouring out her heart before the Lord in prayer.

Christ's heart is said to have ruptured bringing forth the outpouring of blood and water from His body to save ours. Nothing and no one should be more precious to us, for there is none more worthy of our wholehearted devotion, than Him. John 19:34 (NIV) *Instead, one of the soldiers pierced Jesus' side with a spear, bringing a sudden flow of blood and water.*

As the Israelites were turning back to God, who mobilized for attack (verse 7)?

_____

The enemy will pursue to attack that which is valuable to God. Anyone turning to God poses a threat to hell's population. Watch out, beware and on guard but not fearful! (See 1 Peter 5:8 and 1 John 4:4.)

The Israelites pleaded what of Samuel in verse 8?

_____

Don't stop praying!!

Glance back at Eli's question in 1 Samuel 2:25. He wonders who can intercede if someone sins against God… Samuel is God's answer! God will use you to be the answer to someone else's question/prayer as well when you are living wholeheartedly devoted to Him.

I find it both interesting and encouraging that although Samuel was not officially eligible to take the high priest position once Eli and his sons past (because he was not a direct descendant of Aaron), he was the one who was able to act as such at that time. Samuel was the one able to offer the important sacrifices throughout Israel. Samuel's obedience and devotion to God was a defining characteristic that made his legacy for the Lord great.

Maybe you don't have all the qualifications or degrees that humans often look for to validate a person's existence or quality. Know this dear one, God looks at the heart and His opinion trumps all. He can make a way where there is no way because He is The Way! (See 1 Sam. 16:7, Isaiah 43:19, Ps. 77:19, Job 42:2)

Maybe you have heard it said, He doesn't always call the qualified, but He always qualifies the called.

Then I heard the voice of the Lord saying, "Whom shall I send? And who will go for us?" And I said, "Here am I. Send me!" Isaiah 6:8 (NIV)

Dear one, if you have made it this far in the study you have studied HARD. You have spent in-depth time with Him so that He could write His story on the tablet of your heart and mind. You have something to share, to give away to His glory and praise!!

Just as the enemy comes to attack God's people who are engaged in prayer and worship, who shows up and how? What happens? (1 Sam. 7:10)

Wow!!! *What, then, shall we say in response to these things? If God is for us, who can be against us?* Romans 8:31 (NIV)

Exodus 15:3 (NIV) *The LORD is a warrior; the LORD is his name.* 2 Timothy 2:19 (NLT) *But God's truth stands firm like a foundation stone with this inscription: "The LORD knows those who are his," and "All who belong to the LORD must turn away from evil."* Exodus 14:14 (NKJV) *The LORD will fight for you, and you shall hold your peace."*

The Lord's mighty voice thundered from heaven that day throwing their enemy into total confusion so that the Israelites could take the victory!

But thanks be to God, who in Christ always leads us in triumphal procession, and through us spreads the fragrance of the knowledge of him everywhere. 2 Corinthians 2:14 (ESV)

Please record 1 Samuel 7:12 below.

_____

_____

_____

Samuel raised up a stone and called it Ebenezer (which means "the stone of help"), saying: THUS FAR THE LORD HAS HELPED US!!

A rock memorial to the ONLY God who can turn the impossible tide against sure defeat by the enemy!!! Our God proved He is the Resurrection and the Life there was/is no greater impossible tide to ever need turning than that of sin, death and the devil and He alone was able, and He DID!! Oh dear one He has turned the tide for you and for me. The stone was rolled away and His tomb still stands empty to this day! Our God LIVES and we can exclaim in confidence that, THUS FAR THE LORD OUR GOD HAS HELPED US!

Jesus said to her, "I am the resurrection and the life. The one who believes in me will live, even though they die; and whoever lives by believing in me will never die. Do you believe this?" John 11:25-26 (NIV)

L.ife I.n G.od H.olds T.ruth

God makes us brave enough to call out the enemies bluff and able to step forward in the Truth of what He says about us and over our various situations. So stand up, strong in faith and in ever increasing trust in the undefeated Light of Christ!

We were made to carry His victory into the world so walk in the LIGHT of it dear one for He who promised is faithful (Heb. 10:23)! Call out what you already have in Jesus and the enemy will flee! It's there in that God-confident space that nothing will be able to overcome you; it's where you will taste the sweet victory that's been there all along! Praise Him! Oh praise the precious name of Jesus!

So walk set free, in the LIGHT of remembrance... for He is faithful and true, yesterday, today… and forever (Heb. 13:8).

God bless you muchly dear one~

Please record what you would like to remember most from today's study.

_____

_____

_____

_____

...I love you… Isaiah 43:4 (NIV)
~God

Day 4: Circle The Stones

And you shall write very clearly all the words of this law on these stones you have set up." *Deuteronomy 27:8 (NIV)*

Hello dear friend. We are coming to the end and we will part ways but God still goes with you wherever you go! In trying not to cry I remind myself that friendships formed in Jesus never really end, like a circle, friends in Jesus continue through eternity!! *I thank my God every time I remember you.* Philippians 1:3 (NIV) I do! I really do!!

Please bow in prayer before we officially step into His precious Word for our last bit of study together.

Please read 2 Kings 2. ____

Two dear friends are pictured in this passage, Elijah and Elisha. Right away in verse 1 God has made it clear Elijah will be taken to heaven in a whirlwind leaving Elisha to continue on earth.

No matter how much of a warning you have before a good-bye I'm afraid it always seems like a whirlwind, because good-byes are hard and we always seem to be left wishing we had just a bit more time to linger. In Jesus it's not good-bye but rather, "see you soon" and even though "happy" can still elude those moments we have a steadfast joy that remains in the pit to bring light to the heaviness even still. Praise our victorious Savior who LIVES!!

Jesus said to her, "I am the resurrection and the life. The one who believes in me will live, even though they die; and whoever lives by believing in me will never die. Do you believe this?" John 11:25-26 (NIV)

2 Kings 2:1 tells us these two friends were traveling from where?

_____

Gilgal. Gilgal means, circle of stones. Do you remember yesterday's study when Samuel and company experienced a victory? What was it they raised up and what did they name it? (Hint: 1 Samuel 7:12)

_____

Samuel held up a stone and named it "Ebenezer" to stand as a memorial to all that, thus far the Lord had helped them.

In our chapter today (2 Kings 2) we are going to notice two characters, Elijah and Elisha, take a journey. A journey of sorts it would seem, through some "stones of remembrance" that I would imagine emboldened their faith during a difficult time.

If we were to draw a map we might label it "Gilgal" or circle of stones. Now let's begin our journey, circling of the "stones of remembrance" with them!

2 Kings 2:2 seems to parallel Ruth 1:16. Take a moment to compare both addresses and record what you find similar between the response of Ruth and that of Elisha below.

_____

_____

Ruth insists on going to Bethlehem with Naomi. Bethlehem remember means house of bread. Jesus is our Bread of Life. Ruth wants to take Naomi's God (The Bread if Life) as her own. Elisha insists on going to Bethel with Elijah, Bethel means house of God. The Light in Elijah and in Naomi held a brilliant contrast to the world as they knew it and they were not about to part ways. *Follow my example, as I follow the example of Christ.* 1 Corinthians 11:1 (NIV)

In the way we act, think and speak in all our different arenas of life (work, home, recreational…) do we reflect or block the character of Jesus for others to see? Do we portray the sustenance of our life as being Jesus, the Bread of Life? Do we portray that there is nowhere else we would rather be than the house of God (in His presence). Is it apparent that we have made God our dwelling place?

If we were mapping our journey we would now draw a dot and label it Bethel.

Genesis 28:10-22 records a spectacular event that takes place at Bethel. This is the place the patriarch Jacob is recorded to have thought, … *"Surely the Lord is in this place, and I was not aware of it."* (Gen. 28:16 NIV) I wonder if as Elijah and Elisha passed this place, (this "stone of remembrance" we are calling it) did it reminded them that in ALL things God is with them even still, even if, and even when, they can't feel Him?! Feelings are not facts, God's Word is fact… *Have I not commanded you? Be strong and courageous. Do not be afraid; do not be discouraged, for the Lord your God will be with you wherever you go."* Joshua 1:9 (NIV)

2 Kings 2:3 records Elisha telling the other voices to be quiet. Especially in a storm or a trial the voices will rage around you battling for your focus. You don't have to be benched from the playing field of life to be rendered ineffective, just distracted. On the soccer field how helpful is the player that is daydreaming?! God often whispers so you have to lean in close and stay laser focused (1 Kings 19:12-13). *Fixing our eyes on Jesus, the pioneer and perfecter of faith. For the joy set before him he endured the cross, scorning its shame, and sat down at the right hand of the throne of God.* Hebrews 12:2 (NIV) Fix your focus on Jesus, pray His voice be your loudest reality.

In 2 Kings 2:4 what town are Elisha and Elijah headed to?

_____

Jericho. If you completed "TRUST in The Light" with us Jericho will be very familiar to you! Remember Rahab who had a home built into the very wall around the great city of Jericho (Joshua 6)! That wall that crumbled to ash and YET her home remained standing, steadfast and firm because she trusted in God Almighty!! I wonder if passing through this "stone of remembrance" emboldened Elisha and Elijah's faith to trust that their God was a God who brings beauty from ash and joy instead of mourning (Isaiah 61:3)?!

On our imaginary mind map you can add Jericho and a line connecting it to Bethel.

By 2 Kings 2:6 where or what "stone of remembrance", are they coming up on?

_____

The Jordan. In Joshua 3 God parted the Jordan at flood stage so His people could cross on dry ground. However they were required to step in first BEFORE the waters parted! They stepped in faith and found God faithful.

Please read Joshua 4:1-7 and record below what God had them build to remind them and the next generations of His faithfulness?

_____

A 12 stone memorial!! More stones of remembrance! Joshua 4:3 tells us these stones were to be taken from the middle of the Jordan. Often it's in the middle of our storms that we struggle the most to see any sign of hope. We're too far in to turn around and too far out from the other side to see clearly. It's from the middle of a trial that we often need to be reminded the most of God's faithfulness.

Taking stones from the middle would remind them not to get riddled in the middle! God is faithful, He IS the Alpha and the Omega, the Beginning and the End (Rev. 22:13). We can trust the One who is Faithful and True (Rev. 19:11) even in our middles. The One who started your life will carry it on to completion (Phil. 4:6). In Jesus you make it to the other side and you make it safely (2 Timothy 4:18). Some of us might feel as if we're coming in like a flaming cannonball (this world is broken and it hurts), but according to this 2 Timothy promise, I believe we nail the landing with a perfect 10, not even smelling like smoke! Hallelujah!

I'd like to believe that, that 12 stone memorial was still standing there when Elisha and Elijah came upon the Jordan that day and that is what emboldened there faith to do what they did and walk once more through the Jordan on DRY ground!! *The one who calls you is faithful, and he will do it.* 1 Thessalonians 5:24 (NIV)

In 2 Kings 2:9 what does Elisha desire to have that Elisha has?

_____

A double portion of God's Spirit within.

How does Elijah respond to Elisha's question in verse 10?

_____

He says it is a difficult thing. Now we know nothing is difficult for God (Matt. 19:26) so I wonder if what Elijah meant is that it is a difficult thing to bear. To whom much is given much is required (Luke 12:48). We desire "fruit" or good things to come from our lives that honor our God. He promises to produce the fruit if we remain in the Vine (John 15:5). However we often see the "wine" flowing from another's life and desire that, not remembering that sweet wine is produced through a crushing of grapes. We often want the "wine" without the crushing/trials and when we get the crushing/trials, we resist His refining process and whine! Faithfully, His strength is made perfect in our weakness (2 Cor. 12:9) and He never asks us to do anything alone but rather to yoke up to Him for His grace is always sufficient. *"Come to me, all you who are weary and burdened, and I will give you rest. Take my yoke upon you and learn from me, for I am gentle and humble in heart, and you will find rest for your souls. For my yoke is easy and my burden is light."* Matthew 11:28-30 (NIV)

Our mind map should now have three stones of remembrance connected in a half circle. Bethel - Jericho - Jordan…

2 Kings 2:11 reveals just as God promised, Elijah was taken up in a whirlwind. It was by chariot and horses of fire!! Talk about a WILD ride! Walking with Jesus will be anything but dull, that is for sure but He promises us in Isaiah 43:2 (NIV) *When you pass through the waters, I will be with you; and when you pass through the rivers, they will not sweep over you. When you walk through the fire, you will not be burned; the flames will not set you ablaze.* There will be fiery trials but we won't

go through them alone (Jn. 16:33), He will be with us and we WILL arrive safely in our forever home in Heaven, that is a promise! 2 Timothy 4:18 (NIV) *The Lord will rescue me from every evil attack and will bring me safely to his heavenly kingdom. To him be glory for ever and ever. Amen.*

In 2 Kings 2:12 Elisha is crying out for Elijah and he is no more. Sometimes your strong one is taken and that's when you realize The Strong One never leaves and always stands by your side. Your heavenly Father is with you even still, even if, even when…

Elisha, in his grief does a "Gilgal" so to speak, and circles the stones. He goes back to what he knows to find his faith in all the he doesn't. Elisha goes back through the stones of remembrance he just walked with his friend Elijah but this time it is just him. Sometimes God gives us a friend to walk with us and sometimes He takes us down a path with just Himself. *The Lord is my shepherd, I lack nothing. He makes me lie down in green pastures, he leads me beside quiet waters, he refreshes my soul. He guides me along the right paths for his name's sake. Even though I walk through the darkest valley, I will fear no evil, for you are with me; your rod and your staff, they comfort me.* Psalm 23:1-4 (NIV)

In 2 Kings 2:14 (NV) Elisha cry's out at the Jordan *"Where now is the LORD, the God of Elijah?"* God is not afraid of our emotion. *Then you will call on me and come and pray to me, and I will listen to you.* Jeremiah 29:12 (NIV) The same God that brought Joshua and the Israelites across on dry ground and then Elijah, would now be with Elisha and walk him across on dry ground! *Let us hold unswervingly to the hope we profess, for he who promised is faithful.* Hebrews 10:23 (NIV) Don't ever doubt for a moment that He is not with you too. Walk with God, you will make it to the other side, walking all the while on dry ground!

By 2 Kings 2:18 Elisha has made it back to Jericho and by verse 23 he is in Bethel. Elisha circled his stones of remembrance and found God's presence faithfully with Him! God's sustaining strength was enough to make it victoriously through it all!! The God who was faithful to Jacob and Rahab and Joshua and Elijah, was faithful to Elisha and will be faithful to you too, dear one. You were made to carry His victory within you to a desperate world!

We can complete our mind map as it comes full circle. Their journey records a circling of Bethel to Jericho to the Jordan and back through the Jordan to Jericho and to Bethel. God was the constant traveling companion whether the friends were together or not. ...*for the Lord your God will be with you wherever you go.*" (Joshua 1:9 NIV)

I would encourage you to find a small stone and like Samuel named his "Ebenezer" you can write "Victory" on yours. Let this stand as your "stone of remembrance" of all the faithful Truth you have uncovered throughout your study of His Word these past ten weeks. If you have been traveling with us through the other study books in the L.I.G.H.T. series you may want to circle your stones together now. So when you feel like you are becoming riddled in the middle of your "Jordan", go back to your stones of remembrance that remind you of His Truth and faithfulness: "TRUST", "LIVE", "REST", "VICTORY". Go back to what you know to find your faith in all that you don't.

It's not about finding all the answers. In the end you can find your head full of knowledge and your heart still void of healing, significance, hope, love... unless you have allowed yourself to let go into Him. In trusting Him beyond what you can see and comprehend allows you to truly live full in the rest and peace that flows from a vessel filled with His victory.

You were made to be a vessel of His victory!

But thanks be to God, who always leads us as captives in Christ's triumphal procession and uses us to spread the aroma of the knowledge of him everywhere. 2 Corinthians 2:14 (NIV)

…"To him who sits on the throne and to the Lamb be praise and honor and glory and power, for ever and ever!" Revelation 5:13 (NIV)

To him who is able to keep you from stumbling and to present you before his glorious presence without fault and with great joy— to the only God our Savior be glory, majesty, power and authority, through Jesus Christ our Lord, before all ages, now and forevermore! Amen. Jude 1:24-25 (NIV)

Please record the one thing that has impacted your heart the most from your study today.

_____

_____

_____

_____

Day 5: A Time To Reflect

Today is for what you typically have done on day 6 & 7 of your previous weeks of study. There is something extra special planned for your last weeks day 6 & 7 reflection tomorrow. However today take time to reflect over your week of study. Maybe you need some time to catch up on the study material and this might be the perfect break to do just that with the Lord!

I encourage you to glance back at the final point at the end of each day that you recorded having had the greatest impact on your heart. As you spend time with God in prayer, reflect and record on the lines below how God is tying it all together and applying it to your life.

Ask that God make it clear who He would have you invite into a natural opportunity to share Him, to apply what you are learning. Trust Him to continue to take the lead. May we have a heart ever ready with eyes and ears out to the opportunities God wants to invite us into for His glory and praise.

Do not merely listen to the word, and so deceive yourselves. Do what it says. Anyone who listens to the word but does not do what it says is like someone who looks at his face in a mirror and, after looking at himself, goes away and immediately forgets what he looks like. But whoever looks intently into the perfect law that gives freedom, and continues in it - not forgetting what they have heard, but doing it - they will be blessed in what they do. James 1:22-25 (NIV)

_____

_____

_____

_____

_____

Philippians 4:13 (NIV) *I can do all things through him who gives me strength.*

John 14:26 (NIV) *But the Advocate, the Holy Spirit, whom the Father will send in my name, will teach you all things and will remind you of everything I have said to you.*

Day 6 & 7: Raise Your "Ebenezer"!

Hello friend. Today will just be a time for you to go back through the last nine "Day 6 & 7: A Time To Reflect" pages with God. Spend time going over all the Truths He has spoken to your heart and let the Spirit remind, teach and apply as only He can. Let these things you remember or "stones of remembrance" so to speak, stand to remind you always, that thus far the Lord has helped you (1 Samuel 7:12 NIV). May this embolden your faith and trust in our Lord Jesus Christ, who was, is and will continue to be victorious and ever faithful to you.

As you pray and work through things with God please record anything you would like below.

_____

_____

_____

_____

_____

_____

_____

_____

_____

_____

_____

_____

_____

_____

_____

_____

_____

_____

_____

_____

_____

_____

_____

_____

_____

_____

_____

_____

_____

_____

_____

_____

_____

_____

Jesus Christ is the same yesterday and today and forever. Hebrews 13:8 (NIV) So, *Let us hold unswervingly to the hope we profess, for he who promised is faithful.* Hebrews 10:23 (NIV)

Thank you most sincerely and may God bless you oh so very muchly~ Janette

Study Group Discussion Note Space: Weeks 1-10

Therefore, as you received Christ Jesus the Lord, so walk in him, rooted and built up in him and established in the faith, just as you were taught, abounding in thanksgiving. Colossians 2:6-7 (ESV)

ABOUT: Redeeming grace 99|1 Ministries

Redeeming Grace 99|1 Ministries is based on Matthew 18:12-14. There is no situation, circumstance or life God cannot reach, restore, revive and fully redeem for our good and His glory. Redeeming grace is the criminal on the cross entering into Paradise; it's Ruth the pagan becoming part of Jesus' genealogy; it's Jairus' daughter brought back to life; it's Joseph pulled from the prison and made a mighty leader; it's Daniel on the other side of the lion's den; it's Saul turned Paul; it's Jonah out of the whale; it's David and Bathsheba's son Solomon; it's Hannah having Samuel after barrenness; it's the man lame for 38 years made to walk; it's five loaves and two fish becoming a meal feeding 5,000 with leftovers; it's Lazarus walking out of the tomb; it's the widow's oil that never ran out; it's the parting of the Red Sea and the receding of the Jordan; it's you and I realizing our need for a Savior as we look to Jesus high and lifted up, believing His death on the cross was in our place for our sin, then resurrecting from the grave God defeating the enemy of our souls once and for all. We are made new in receiving the transforming Truth of His love so that we might be made a vessel of His victory. His redeeming grace writes living hope on every page of our lives. You have never laid eyes on someone God did not love. Our mission is to reach one, and then another and another...with the Good News of His redeeming grace for us all through Jesus, raising the population of heaven by His grace, to His glory and praise.

Redeeming Grace 99|1 Ministries
graphic designs © 2020 Design credit: Noah Kieffer

Author headshot photo credit: Jesse and Laura Rogers

ABOUT THE AUTHOR

By God's amazing grace, Janette resides in Colorado with her husband (married in 2003) their six children and lovable dog named Brave. As a teacher by trade, she finds joy in learning and sharing her passion for the hope filled Word of God. Find other books by Janette Kieffer on Amazon such as...

"Reigning in the Rain" is a one year devotional study journal that will encourage you to see Living Hope on every page of your life.

"TRUST in The Light" is book one in a 4 part series called L.I.G.H.T. (Life In God Holds Truth). This series studies the life of Jesus through the harmony of the four gospels. Go back to what you know to find your faith in all that you do not. Allow God to use your questions, doubts, fears, failures, even your triumphs as tools to bring Truth into the Light. Truth you never would have known otherwise. With the rock of ever-increasing TRUST lay the first steppingstone of your faith on the firm foundation of the Faithful and True. He is the same yesterday, today and forever. In an ever-changing world come delight yourself in the Light of God's love for you that will not falter, fail or fade. TRUST in the Light.

"LIVE in The Light" is book two in the L.I.G.H.T. series. This 10 week study book takes us further into the life of Jesus. Upon the solid foundation of Christ we place our trust that we may truly step into life as He intended it to be lived. In a world with ever fluctuating standards of validation, come delight yourself in Him who remains unchanging and steadfast throughout he ages. Through His life we learn to live with great expectancy rather than tangled and tripped up in our faulty expectations. Come step into the Light of His lavish love for you and LIVE!

"REST in The Light" Who understands insanely busy and intense life pressures more than Jesus?! Our God sweat drops of blood in the Garden of Gethsemane in prayer over the severe burden He was enduring on our behalf! Yet at the end of that prayer as the enemy approached Jesus stood and said, "Arise, let's go." not, "Arise let's panic and run!". Our God victoriously faced head on the rush of this world resting in The Father. In this part three of the L.I.G.H.T. series we will embark through another 10 weeks of study diving ever deeper into the life of Christ through the harmony of the four gospels (Matthew, Mark, Luke and John). In a world that spins on busy and runs on filtered picture-perfect displays of altered reality, come rest your heart in the nail scarred palm of the true Prince of Peace. REST in God and let Him build His authentic purpose through you. God only builds beautiful things that display His splendor. A seed in the soil just rests, it rests even when it's dark, cold and dirty; it remains still, trusting the process…They are the shoot I have planted, the work of my hands, for the display of my splendor. Isaiah 60:21 (NIV) God builds, God plants, God works, and by His amazing grace God will make us a display of His splendor if only we will stay RESTING in His mighty capable and trustworthy hands. REST, trust His process and grow to truly live in His victory! …"Come with me by yourselves to a quiet place and get some rest." ~Jesus (Mark 6:31 NIV)

May the God of hope fill you with all joy and peace as you trust in him, so that you may overflow with hope by the power of the Holy Spirit. Romans 15:13 (NIV)

Made in the USA
Columbia, SC
13 May 2021

3741/485R00141